P9-CTB-034

The Old Cathedral

BY

GREGORY M. FRANZWA

Archdiocese of St. Louis

1965

DEDICATION

This book is dedicated to the pioneers of another era—the St. Louisans of today. In the face of 50 years of discouragement, delay and decay, they gave sacrificially of their time and, in some cases, their money, to bring about a rebirth of the spirit of St. Louis. Because of these few dozen citizens, a renaissance has been triggered which has resulted in new buildings of handsome architecture, new commerce and industry, new political integrity, and a new spirit in the hearts of their fellow citizens. They will not be enshrined in the annals of history with Marquette and Joliet, Lewis and Clark, or LaSalle. But as long as the great arch stands, they will not be forgotten.

✝   ✝   ✝

ACKNOWLEDGMENT

The author is indebted to Rev. John Francis Bannon, S.J., whose penetrating criticism of the original draft of this narrative has been most helpful. (Father Bannon is Chairman of the History Department of St. Louis University.)

The careful reading and commentary of Rev. Bernard E. Granich, Archdiocesan Archivist, is also acknowledged with gratitude.

FOREWORD

The Old Cathedral is more than the story of our famous old church on the downtown riverfront—it is the story of man, his church, his God, and his epic struggle against the frontier. It is a continuing story. The frontiers, no less formidable, now are of the intellect. It will be the task of other men in other eras to pass judgement upon our contemporary struggle to achieve a better community of man. Let us hope the heroism described in this book will provide added inspiration to those charged with this massive responsibility.

Joseph Cardinal Ritter

TABLE OF CONTENTS

INDEX TO ILLUSTRATIONS

The
Old
Cathedral

Nihil Obstat: RT. REV. WILLIAM M. DRUMM, P.A., J.C.D.
Censor Librorum

Imprimatur: JOSEPH CARDINAL RITTER
Archbishop of St. Louis
September 1, 1965

Chapter I

GREAT EXPLORATIONS IN THE MIDDLE VALLEY

The old church never looked better. It had a new coat of paint on the ancient walls; the handsome Georgian windows had been restored. Cool air flooded the nave on a muggy day. The walnut beams above the vaulted ceiling had been strapped with steel—the same beams that were saplings three centuries ago when they stood on the silent limestone bluff high above the Mississippi.

There were 400 people in the church that Friday morning, September 20, 1963. They were there not so much in celebration of the completion of the exhaustive rehabilitation program begun four years before. They were there to observe a formal announcement by Joseph Cardinal Ritter; the Old Cathedral no longer was to be called the Church of St. Louis IX, King of France. Now it was the Basilica of St. Louis, the King. The Basilican status had been decreed by Pope John XXIII on January 27, 1961. Only a few churches in the world have higher honors than the Old Cathedral.

✝   ✝   ✝

So much was written in the Bicentennial years of the founding of St. Louis that hundreds of thousands of St. Louisans are aware of the historic events of 1764. Few realize, however, that much history had passed before Laclede's command to Chouteau: "You will come here as soon as navigation opens and will cause this place to be cleared, in order to form our settlement after the plan that I shall give you."

Some 130 years before the voyage of Marquette and Joliet, the Spanish conquistador Hernando de Soto and his band of adventurers, flushed with the conquest of Peru and swollen with ransomed gold of the Inca, landed in Florida. De Soto had no reason to believe that similar civilizations and like treasures did not exist in the northern hemisphere, and began his search in the land that had done Ponce de Leon to his death. For two years De Soto followed a tortuous route to the American Southwest, finally crossing the great Mississippi just below what is now Memphis. He pursued a northerly course, along the west bank of the river, in what was to become the St. Louis Diocese. He died the following year, broken and discouraged, and was committed to the river he discovered.

Simultaneously Francisco Vasquez de Coronado was on a similar mission in the mid-continent, searching for the golden city of Quivira. He found it in central Kansas, the temporary habitat of nomadic Indians, living in shelters of poles and buffalo hides.

Both great adventures are important to the history of the Old Cathedral, because both areas lie within the borders of what was to become the Diocese of St. Louis. Both are important because they illustrate the role of the Catholic Priest in the opening of the American West.

De Soto bore with him a coterie of clergy—twelve priests, eight brothers, and four monks. Coronado brought four friars with him, a number which had diminished to one by the time he reached his fabled city. It was during the return trek, in April of 1542, that Fray Juan de Padilla received permission to return to teach the Quivira Indians.

Such was the zeal of Padilla that he elected to spread his faith among neighboring tribes, an act considered traitorous by the Quivira and as spying by the others. He encountered a band of Indians on the warpath, and after first seeing that his companions had fled to safety, knelt in the path to receive a fusillade of arrows. His body was interred in a pit and covered with boulders. A brief flash of light in a dark continent.

The first of the English colonies was established in Virginia in 1607, and the following year the French were in Quebec.

✝ ✝ ✝

The exploration of most singular importance to the American mid-continent undoubtedly was the voyage of Joliet and Marquette. Although their southernmost penetration was only 100 miles below Memphis, at the mouth of the Arkansas river, they definitely established that the great river indeed emptied into the ocean, thus affording access to the heart of the continent by water. (The maps of that day had indicated that the Gulf of California might be the southern terminus of the Mississippi.)

JACQUES MARQUETTE

Jacques Marquette was a 36-year-old Jesuit priest in 1673, the year the expedition left the Mission of St. Ignace at Michilimakinac. Louis Joliet was only 28. The two and their companions paddled their canoes down the western shore of Lake Michigan to Green Bay, fought the currents up the Fox River, portaged to the Wisconsin near the Dells and some days later, on June 17, 1673, they floated out onto the Mississippi. The pair had good cause for elation—they had only the word of itinerant Indians that the river extended that far north.

That Marquette, the chronicler of the adventure, was a man of peace did not mean he was not also a man of caution. The following is a quotation from his journal:

"We continued to advance, but as we knew not whither we were going . . . we kept on our guard. On this account we made only a small fire on land, toward evening, to cook our meals; and, after supper, we remove ourselves as far from it as possible, and pass the night in our canoes, which we anchor in the river at some distance from the shore."

Nor were they men of little courage: "On the 25th of June, we perceived on the water's edge some tracks of men, and a narrow and somewhat beaten path leading to a fine prairie. We stopped . . . thinking that it was a road which led to some village of savages, we resolved to go and reconnoiter it . . . We silently followed the narrow path, and after walking about two leagues (six miles), we discovered a village on the bank of a river, and two others on a hill distant . . . We therefore decided that it was time to reveal ourselves. This we did by shouting with all our energy, and stopped, without advancing any farther."

The Indians of the Illinois happened to be friendly and Marquette was familiar with their dialect. The encounter took place on the north bank of the mouth of the Des Moines river, where Keokuk now is located.

He makes pointed reference in his journals of the Piasa bird near Alton: "While skirting some rocks, which by their height and length inspired awe, we saw upon one of them two painted monsters, which at first made us afraid . . . They are as large as a calf; they

3

have horns on their heads . . . a horrible look, red eyes, a beard like a tiger's, a face somewhat like a man's, a body covered with scales, and so long a tail that it winds all around the body, passing above the head and going back between the legs, ending in a fish's tail."

Although the cliff has been chipped away by time and the highway builders, the Piasa bird has been re-painted in approximately the same spot, some 19 miles upstream from St. Louis, just northwest of the city of Alton.

No sooner had the explorers recovered from this than they came upon the confluence of the Missouri, just north of the limits of what today is the City of St. Louis, and the Chain of Rocks, just downstream: "While sailing quietly in clear and calm water, we heard the noise of a rapid, into which we were about to run. I have seen nothing more dreadful. An accumulation of large and entire trees, branches, and floating islands, was issuing from the mouth of the river Pekitanoui, with such impetuosity that we could not, without great danger, risk passing through it. So great was the agitation that the water was very muddy, and could not become clear."

Days later, after the party had suffered several narrow escapes from savages on the warpath (and since the stock of provisions was becoming low), they turned their canoes into the current near the mouth of the Arkansas, secure in the knowledge that the river continued to salt water. They elected to return to Lake Michigan via the Illinois river, leaving the Mississippi some 28 miles northwest of St. Louis. Along the river they found a village of the Illinois, called Kaskaskia, consisting of 74 cabins. The Indians extracted from Marquette a promise that he would return to instruct them. He did so three days before Easter, 1675, thus founding the first mission in the Mississippi valley—Immaculate Conception, near Starved Rock state park.

The arduous voyage had wreaked havoc with Marquette's health. He elected to return to his home mission at St. Ignace. With the life slipping out of him, Marquette and his two Indian companions pulled into a little river (Pere Marquette), where, at the age of 38, he gave up the ghost.

But in those few years Marquette had supplied an abundance of inspiration to the Catholic missionaries that was not to ebb until the wild continent was subdued. Indeed, it still continues in remote outposts of the world. (The St. Louis Archdiocese currently main-

4

tains missions in Bolivia and Chile, and religious communities from the Archdiocese serve in a number of other missions in South America.)

As Marquette was fired by a zeal to convert the savages of the Illinois country to Christianity, Robert Cavelier, sieur de La Salle, was possessed of an immense determination to claim the valley of the Mississippi for France. It was his goal to lay a string of French fortifications from Lake Ontario to the Gulf, to protect the territory from the English threat. It was also his goal to capitalize upon his letters patent, giving him exclusive rights to the fur trade along the river. With three French Recollects, he set out in 1682 to claim the land for his sovereign, Louis XIV, in honor of whom he gave it the name, Louisiana.

One of the priests, Louis Hennepin, ascended the river as far as the Falls of St. Anthony (St. Paul, Minnesota). The other two, following in Marquette's footsteps, set about establishing missions and giving instructions as they descended the river. On April 6, 1682, they reached the delta and tidewater. There they erected a column on which they inscribed, "Louis the Great, King of France and Navarre, reigns; the 9th of April, 1682."

LaSalle returned to Quebec the following spring, then departed to communicate directly with the French court. He was given four vessels with which to find the mouth of the Mississippi by sea. His faithful companion, the one-armed Henri de Tonti, returned to the delta to await the arrival of LaSalle. But LaSalle fell victim to the unfortunate map-making techniques of the day and landed some 400 miles to the west, mistaking the dead-end Matagorda bay, south of Galveston, for the mouth of the Mississippi. His only remaining vessel sank there, and he had no recourse but to seek the river by land. He proceeded northeast for three months with a band of 20 men. As spirits sank deeper, on March 19, 1687, he was murdered from ambush by two of his own men. The loyal remnants of the party eventually reached Quebec.

Tonti, who had waited at the delta several weeks, finally elected to return to the north. But he paused at the mouth of the Arkansas long enough to lay the foundations of Arkansas Post, destined to become an important stopover between New Orleans and St. Louis.

Chapter II

BLACK ROBES IN THE ILLINOIS COUNTRY

Although only a handful of St. Louisans are aware of it, Laclede and Chouteau were far from being the first white men to see the white limestone rise that was to become St. Louis. It is not inconceivable that Marquette and Joliet might have stopped below the grove of walnut trees that commanded the river. LaSalle most likely cast more than a lingering glance at the easily-defendable eminence, just below the confluence of the Missouri. It is a certainty that the three "Gentlemen of the Seminary" said Mass on the site on December 8, 1698, 65 years before Laclede first laid eyes on the bluff. What is a little surprising is that somebody didn't develop the potential before Laclede.

✝   ✝   ✝

François Joliet de Montigny, Antoine Davion, and Jean François Buisson de St. Cosme, missionary priests from the Seminary of Quebec, left accounts in 1694 of their visit to Francis Pinet, priest of the Mission of the Guardian Angel, located on the banks of the Chicago river at Lake Michigan. St. Cosme: "We went ... to the house of the Reverend Jesuit Fathers ... found there Pinet and Binneteau. Their house is built on the bank of a small river, with the lake on one side and a fine and vast prairie on the other. The village of the savages contains over 150 cabins, and a league up the river is still another village almost as large."

The three were sent by their Bishop to establish missions in the country of the Illinois. They were more than a little surprised to find this task already well underway by a number of Jesuits along the Illinois river. The Black Robes, too, were surprised and probably a little put out by this "invasion" of the clerics from the North. The rights of the first arrivals were duly recognized, however; the three reverend gentlemen set out for points south, there being no abundance of missionaries on the Mississippi itself.

On December 3, 1698, a heavy gale broke up the ice and the trio moved out of the mouth of the Illinois and onto the Father of Waters.

The missionaries were accompanied by Tonti (who had been La Salle's chief lieutenant), and who was suspected of being a gun-runner to the enemies of the harassed Illinois tribes. Tonti counseled with the Indians at Cahokia, while the Gentlemen of the Seminary repaired to the west bank, near the foot of Arsenal Street, where they erected a stone altar. There, a few hundred yards below the spot where Laclede would land, each in turn offered Mass. It was the morning of December 8, 1698, the Feast of the Immaculate Conception.

The three reached the villages of the Arkansas Indians at Tonti's Arkansas Post, and from there each returned to separate Indian villages to assume the roles of resident missionaries.

Their voyage is of little consequence in itself, except that it was one of the few of that day which was richly documented. It served as a supplement to the journals of Marquette, and as the first direct and positive identification of the site that was to become St. Louis.

The mission at Cahokia, four miles south of St. Louis, was founded in 1699 by Jean Bergier, another of the Seminary priests of Quebec. In 1700, St. Cosme returned to that mission. Some years later he was murdered by a war party of Chitimacha Indians. Pierre de Iberville, one of the colonizers of the Lower Mississippi, apprehended and executed the guilty chiefs.

✝   ✝   ✝

The Cahokias, Kaskaskias and Tamarois (pronounced "Tamaroa") tribes of the Illinois nation, located on the site of the present town of Cahokia, had been subject to repeated harassment by the marauding Sioux from the northwest, and especially by the Shawnees from the southeast.

One such raid illustrates not only the savagery of the attacking war party, but the long way the missionaries had to go before they could truly refer to their charges as "civilized."

Bergier leaves this account of an attack, written June 14, 1700: "We have frequent alarms here, and have several times been obliged to receive within our walls nearly all the women and children of the village. Pentecost Sunday there was an alarm, which was not without consequences. Some Sioux war party had murdered a number of men and women. Some Tamarois Indians and Frenchmen fought off the invaders and captured three Sioux. The prisoners were killed, burnt and eaten." Pinet delivered instructions to one of the victims, baptising him just before his demise. As the raids intensified at the close of the year 1700, both tribes resolved to seek more peaceable homes to the south. The great Illinois Black Robe of that day, Jacques

7

Gravier, set out to find such lands. Gabriel Marest, pastor of the Kaskaskia, and Pinet (Chicago's first resident priest), who served the Tamarois, left a few weeks later. They floated down the Mississippi late that year, encountering such severity of the weather that they put into the mouth of a small stream on the west bank to await better weather or the return of Gravier. This little French and Indian community thus became the first civilized outpost in Missouri's history.

The river shortly became known as "La Riviere Des Peres," or river of the Fathers, now little more than a concreted drainage ditch forming the southern boundary of the City of St. Louis. The mission was called St. François Xavier.

✝   ✝   ✝

The Kaskaskias left River Des Peres sometime in 1703 to establish their permanent home at the mouth of the Kaskaskia river, about 50 miles south of St. Louis in Randolph county, Illinois. The new village grew, as the Indians evidently found the peace they sought. It became a center of middle-river activity until the rapid growth of St. Louis caused its decline. The settlement lasted, however, until the uncontrolled waters of the two rivers washed it into oblivion. More than 3,000 bodies were removed from the cemetery in 1892 and 1893, as the water encroached on the final acreage of the old town.

Kaskaskia in its prime evidently was a settlement of some great substance. There were no courts, no lawyers, no taxes or jails—only the Blackrobe Marest. Quite a number of Canadians populated the village, and a number of French. White girls were sent from French convents to be given in marriage to worthy Frenchmen.

Within 20 years of its founding, Kaskaskia became the center of a cluster of villages. Fort Chartres was built in 1720 by the Commandant in Illinois, about 16 miles northwest of the mission. Shortly thereafter a church was built nearby, the Parish of St. Anne of Fort Chartres.

Prairie du Rocher dates to 1734, when St. Joseph's Mortuary Chapel was erected 11 miles northwest, on the bluffs. The town still survives. The village and church of St. Philippe was built just northeast of Fort Chartres in 1723 by Philippe François Renault, Director General of the mining operations of the Royal Company of the Indies. A good road connected this complex of villages with the Parish of the Holy Family in Cahokia, 45 miles to the north.

8

Sometime in 1720, the seat of the government of the colony moved to Fort Chartres. The in-migration of the French brought troubles, and the peace so coveted by the Kaskaskias began to slip from their grasp. Sixteen years later, the military commandant was advised by his superiors in New Orleans to assemble a war party to attack the Chickasaws, who allegedly had been harassing colonists some miles below Kaskaskia. A company of French militia, a group of Miami Indians, the Cahokias,

THE EARLY SETTLEMENTS

Mitchigameas and the Kaskaskias exercised their war dances, and the expedition left in February of 1736.

The Chickasaws were ready and waiting. The expected reinforcements from New Orleans and Poste des Arkansas did not materialize. The Miamis betrayed the northern force, and the Illinois and the Missouris ran away. The French and the Kaskaskia marched to their massacre. Fifteen were taken prisoners, including the Jesuit, Senat. When an expected ransom was not forthcoming, the Indians preserved one of their captives as a witness, subjected the rest to torture and eventual death at the stake.

✝   ✝   ✝

The last major settlement in the middle valley, preceding St. Louis, was that of Ste. Genevieve, 46 miles below. The original site was about three miles downstream from the present town, on the alluvial banks of the river. Much of it has long since made its contribution to the delta. The settlement was not spontaneous, as were so many of the early outposts. Probably the founding was in 1734 or 1735, although there is some inconclusive evidence that it might have been as early as 1732. Miners from Kaskaskia probably remained on the site for growing periods of time, until it became evident that the

9

shipments of the heavy ore could be dispatched downriver as well from the west bank (Ste. Genevieve) as the east (Kaskaskia). The exact date of the settlement is unknown because there most likely was no exact date.

It is probable that the French, aware of royal dissatisfaction with the value of the peltry being taken from the valley, encouraged development of the mineral resources. That the hills beyond Ste. Genevieve produced only minute traces of silver must have proved a bitter disappointment to the court of Louis XV. It was only a matter of time, however, before the richness of the lead, salt, lime and iron gave firm foundation for the establishment of a settlement, and that was the beginning of Ste. Genevieve.

As of 1763, the world had yet to learn of the wisdom of the separation of the powers of church and state. Church-state collaboration did have its advantages—some of the first priests to serve the infant village of St. Louis were paid by the Spanish crown, thus allowing them to forego temporal matters and concentrate on civilizing the inhabitants. But it also had its disadvantages, as most graphically illustrated in 1763 by a hare-brained act of the French monarchy—the banishment of the Jesuits.

For some years there had been a vicious and unrelenting campaign against the Jesuits in Europe, centered in the Latin countries. In 1774, Pope Clement XIV capitulated to the pressures of European royalty and ordered the suppression of the Jesuits throughout the Church, an edict to stand until revoked by Pope Pius VII in 1814. Thus, what little civilization had taken place in Upper Louisiana during nearly a century of toil and devotion by the missionary priests, could have gone down the drain. Tiny colonies which had been begging for a pastor for years had to be denied. Indeed, there were many large settlements left with no priest at all, no means of supplying from within the stimulus for maintenance of law and order.

What few belongings the Jesuits had were sold at auction, and they were provided funds for their passage to France. There, they were pensioned from the funds brought from the sale of their possessions.

Thus, the six dejected Black Robes who had served the middle valley so well departed for New Orleans in 1763.

One of their number, Sebastian Meurin, was sufficiently per-

10

suasive to be given the opportunity to return, but not in the role of a Jesuit. He arrived in Ste. Genevieve just a few weeks after Chouteau set his band of workmen after the walnut trees on the bluff across from Cahokia.

Until his arrival there remained but one priest in all the middle valley, the Recollect, Luc Callet, hiding from the British at Cahokia.

Chapter III

ST. LOUIS UNDER THREE FLAGS

It is a fact that every major expedition in upper Louisiana to 1763 either was accompanied by a Catholic priest, or was indeed composed of Catholic priests. It is all the more ironic that Pierre Laclede Liguest, then 40, and 14-year-old Auguste Chouteau, on their way to the mouth of the Missouri, must have passed the despairing band of Jesuits.

PIERRE LACLEDE
LIGUEST
*From a painting by
Fred Conway*

In 1762, Gilbert Antoine de St. Maxent, a wealthy New Orleans merchant, and Laclede were granted exclusive trading rights with the Indians in the Missouri Valley for eight years, by appointment of the French Governor General at New Orleans. On August 3, 1763, their expedition headed up the Mississippi, laden with a vast store of articles to be traded for the peltry.

The party arrived at Ste. Genevieve early in November, but Laclede found no magazine there large enough for the storage of his merchandise. He crossed over to Fort de Chartres. While there was ample storage space there, he concluded that the 80 miles of water separating the fort from the mouth of the Missouri would be entirely too formidable, that the post must be situated at or near the confluence.

Laclede enjoyed the hospitality of the commandant, Noyon de Villiers, then set out with young Chouteau to find a suitable site for a trading post for Maxent-Laclede & Company.

Only a cursory glance at the black and fertile soil of Columbia Bottoms revealed that the confluence was subject to frequent inundation—it obviously was no place for the post.

Slowly they drifted back downstream, scanning the banks. Some 15 miles from the Missouri they were attracted by a shelf of white stone along the bank. They climbed the little bluff where they found the grove of walnut trees. To the southwest were handsome woodlands, to the northwest was a broad prairie. After blazing a number of trees to mark the spot, they returned to Fort de Chartres to commit their plan to paper.

Workmen were recruited from the townspeople of Fort de Chartres, Kaskaskia, and environs, and late in the afternoon of

February 14, 1764, Chouteau and his band arrived at the site. The next day, woodmen felled the trees and temporary shelters were erected.

The first of the permanent buildings to be erected was the warehouse for the storage of the goods and skins. The quarters at Chartres had to be vacated before the English arrived in the Spring. Under the terms of the Treaty of Paris, signed in 1763, the English were ceded all lands east of the Mississippi. They weren't about to afford a French trader free storage facilities. Chouteau had just finished erecting cabins for his workmen when Laclede arrived, early in April. He named his town after the sainted Louis IX.

Laclede staked out the lots—a block for his home and warehouse, a block immediately to the west for church and graveyard purposes. This latter block is the only one of the original tracts which has never changed hands. The Basilica of St. Louis, the King—the Old Cathedral —still stands on that hallowed ground.

A party of Frenchmen paddled over from Cahokia, probably consumed with curiosity about what was going on over there. They found the enthusiasm infectuous; they decided to stay. A large, friendly but heavy-handed band of Missouri Indians also arrived on the scene, and the French changed their minds rather suddenly, returning to Cahokia. Laclede, who had journeyed back to Fort de Chartres to arrange for the loading of the goods, hastened back to the site to restore order.

The youthful Chouteau displayed an amazing maturity in his analysis of the political repercussions of the Treaty of Paris. There was much bitterness on the other side of the river, populated almost exclusively by French and Indians. The French felt no allegiance whatever to George III, and were fully prepared to depart for New Orleans to escape his rule. Yet, they loved the middle valley. Chouteau personally persuaded a number of families to leave Cahokia, Fort de Chartres, Kaskaskia and St. Phillipe, to settle in St. Louis, where they believed they could live out their days under the Lilies of France. Although the secret Treaty of Fontainebleau left the west side of the river to Spain, Philip IV had demonstrated no intent to assume control, and evidently was to leave command with the French. Even if Spain were to assume active control, the French settlers felt they still would be better off than if they were under the thumb of the hated British protestants. The astute Chouteau not only offered them choice lands in his settlement, but provided the conveyances to transport their goods.

By the time Chouteau's effort was concluded, nothing was left of Fort de Chartres except the garrison, which would be gone in the Summer. Quoting Chouteau, "The village of Nouvelle Chartres with the chapel of St. Anne, lay in ruins, the departing villagers having taken along the boards, the windows and the door frames and everything else they could transport to the places where they intended to settle."

✝   ✝   ✝

There isn't a single record to indicate that a Catholic priest visited St. Louis prior to 1766. It is probable, though, that the energetic Luc Callet paddled across the river on a few occasions to care for his former parishioners who migrated to St. Louis. Callet died suddenly, just before the British arrived, in the Fall of 1765. He was 49 years old, and had been in the Illinois country just four years. It is regrettable that no records were left to verify the Franciscan claim that he was the first priest of St. Louis. He is interred at Prairie du Rocher.

Neyon de Villiers struck his colors in October, and the Flag of England flew over Fort de Chartres. M. de Neyon's lieutenant, Saint-Ange de Bellerive, crossed over to St. Louis, where at Laclede's request he assumed authority.

The determined Meurin arrived in Kaskaskia in May of 1764, then crossed over to Ste. Genevieve to become pastor of that growing settlement. The first recorded act of the missionary priest in St. Louis is this first baptismal entry, now held in the rectory of The Old Cathedral:

> "I, the undersigned Missionary Priest of the Parish of St. Louis, baptized under condition, Marie in a tent in Default of a Church; born on . . . . day of the month of September, 1765. Daughter of Jean Baptiste Des Champs and Marie Pion, the father and mother. The Godfather is . . . Rene Tierlerot and the Godmother Marie . . . In testimony of which I have signed with the Godfather:
>
> S. L. Meurin, Priest"

RECORD OF FIRST BAPTISM IN ST. LOUIS,
SEPTEMBER, 1766, WHICH OCCURRED
IN A TENT.

Meurin continued to make records at frequent intervals until May, 1768. It was sixteen months from that time before any further entries were made by a priest.

Among the conditions attached to the permit for Meurin's return to Upper Louisiana were his agreement to accept the New Orleans Capuchins as his superiors, and that he accept no command from the Jesuits. He agreed to this, with the stipulation that Upper Louisiana indeed was no longer within the diocese of Quebec.

But the expulsion of the Jesuits wrought untold hardships on Meurin. The trek to the villages around Kaskaskia was tiring, and the long journey to Cahokia and St. Louis could not be made frequently enough. Meurin committed a serious tactical error by appealing to Quebec for missionary help.

Bishop Briand of Quebec responded not with a contingent of missionaries, but with the appointment as Vicar-General of the Illinois country, including New Orleans, an honor which Meurin decidedly did not need. The news of the appointment reached New Orleans. This was viewed as rank insubordination by the clergy in New Orleans, and as downright treasonous by the Spanish authorities. Fortunately, Meurin was warned. He went into hiding in British territory in 1768.

Noting the foundations of the buildings at Fort de Chartres were crumbling as the Mississippi waters moved ever closer, Meurin removed the bodies of Callet and another pastor, Joseph Gagnon, to the safety of his new home in exile, Prairie du Rocher.

Briand of Quebec soon was able to respond in more positive

ways to the appeal of the 61-year-old Meurin, and in 1768 sent Pierre Gibault to the Illinois country. Gibault, then 31, took over in Kaskaskia, and quite regularly visited the French Catholics of St. Louis. In all probability, it was Gibault who blessed the first church there, in 1770.

The young priest evidently was a dynamo. He moved constantly — from Kaskaskia to Ste. Genevieve to Cahokia to St. Louis to Prairie du Rocher—even to Post Vincennes, 145 miles due east of St. Louis on the Wabash. It was a difficult trip, across swamps with danger on every side. He wrote: "I am always armed with my gun and a pair of pistols against any possible attack."

The great respect the French held for Gibault, and his familiarity with the country, were to pay off handsomely in just a few years in the cause of the American Revolution.

PIERRE GIBAULT

✝   ✝   ✝

Laclede's Village stretched across the riverfront in four tiers. The first street was named the Rue Royale. Then the Rue De L'eglise, then the Rue des Granges, and finally a limestone ridge forming the western limits of the city.

The central east-west axis was Rue Bonhomme (now Market), with Rue de la Tour (Walnut) paralleling a block to the south. The west wall of the Old Cathedral runs along what was once Rue des Granges, and is now a depressed expressway constructed to bring millions of visitors a year to the Jefferson National Expansion Memorial. The Old Cathedral fronts on the street once known as Rue de la Tour. The church lot was separated from the river by the block occupied by Laclede. There were nine east-west streets on each side of the church block. By 1774, there were 15 stone houses and about 100 of vertical logs, their chinks filled with mortar or clay.

There were two areas of commonfields, lands worked by all the citizens, who shared equally in the benefits. Both were fenced

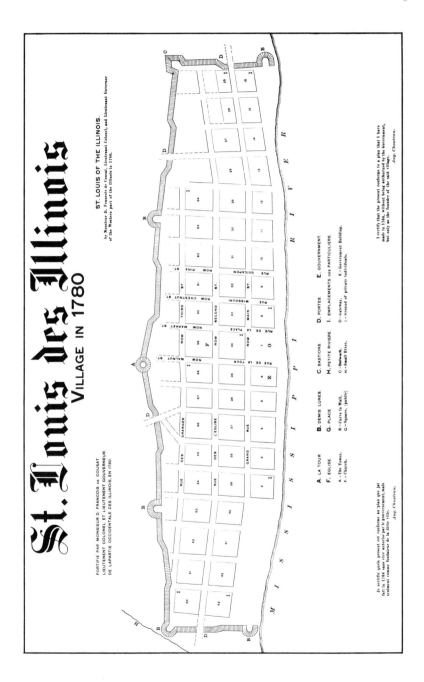

St. Louis des Illinois

VILLAGE IN 1780

FORTIFIE PAR MONSIEUR D. FRANCOIS de COUSAT
LIEUTENANT COLONEL ET LIEUTENENT GOUVERNEUR
DE LAPARTIE OCCIDENTALE DES ILLINOIS, EN 1780

ST. LOUIS OF THE ILLINOIS.
by Monsieur D. Francois de Cousat, Lieutenant Colonel, and Lieutenant Governor
of the Western part of the Illinois in 1780.

A. LA TOUR   B. DEMIS LUNES.   C. BASTIONS.   D. PORTES.   E. GOVERNMENT

F. EGLISE   G. PLACE   H. PETITE RIVIERE.   I. EMPLACEMENTS des PARTICULIERS.

A.=The Tower.   B.=Curve in Wall.   C.=Bulwark.   D.=Gateway.   E.=Government Building.
F.=Church.   G.=Square. (public)   H.=Small River.   I.=Ground of private individuals.

Je certifie qu'le present est conforme au plan que jai
fait in 1764 sans etre autorise par le gouvernment, mais
seulment comme fondateur de la ditte ville.
Aug. Chouteau.

I certify that the present conforms to a plan that I have
made in 1764, without being authorized by the Government,
but only as the founder of the said village.
Aug. Chouteau.

in that first industrious year. The land to the northwest, stretching from Market to a large Indian mound to the north, was cleared of its few trees and placed under cultivation. The land to the south, largely wooded, served as pasture for the town's livestock.

✞   ✞   ✞

The transfer of Louisiana from France to Spain first was felt by St. Louisans in 1770, the year of the arrival of Don Pedro Piernas, lieutenant governor of Upper Louisiana. In 1772, the Capuchin Friar Valentine Neufchateau established himself in St. Louis, not so much as a pastor but more of a chaplain to the Spanish garrison. Still, the St. Louisans were grateful. A military chaplain was better than no priest at all.

One of Pierna's first acts was the building of a church. It was a small rectangular building built of logs, with a roof of clapboards, built facing east on the northeast corner of the lot. It was located on a line between the northeast corner of the rectory of The Old Cathedral, about 150 yards toward the north leg of the Gateway Arch. It was blessed on June 24, 1770, by Gibault.

FIRST CHURCH IN ST. LOUIS—IT FACED EAST, ON NORTHEAST
CORNER OF CHURCH LOT.

It was Valentine who officiated in a colorful ceremony, the baptism of "Pierre Joseph Felicite," a bell for the church. The bell, allegedly enriched by the addition of 200 Spanish pieces of eight, was a gift of Lt. Governor and Senora Piernas. Valentine's record follows:

"In the year 1774, the twenty-fourth of December, I the undersigned have baptized with the ordinary ceremonies of the Church a new bell which was named Pierre Joseph Felicite, and the godfather of which was the Honorable Pierre Joseph de Piernace, captain in the Louisiana battalion, and lieutenant governor of the Illinois, and the godmother,

FIRST CHURCH BELL (1774) STILL HANGS IN OLD CATHEDRAL MUSEUM.

Lady Felicite de Piernace de Portneuf, who have signed with me, the day and year as above."

Pedro Piernas
Felicite Portneuf Piernas
Baron Benito Basquez
Father Valentine, Priest.

Prior to the arrival of Pierre Joseph Felicite, the people had been called to worship by an iron mortar beaten by a heavy iron pestle.

✝   ✝   ✝

So impressive was the growth of the infant village that it was raised to the status of canonical parish in 1776, receiving its first pastor, the Capuchin Bernard de Limpach. He was installed May 19, 1776 by Don Francisco Cruzat, who had replaced Piernas in 1775. Bernard immediately celebrated Mass in the four-year-old log church, which even then was falling apart.

✝   ✝   ✝

19

He then set about the task of replacing the dilapidated church and the construction of a new rectory.

SECOND CHURCH (1776) WAS BUILT ON SECOND STREET, HALF WAY BETWEEN WALNUT AND MARKET.

On December 26, 1774, the inhabitants of the town met in the chambers of Don Piernas and discussed the plan for a second church. It was to be 60 feet by 30 feet, girdled by a five-foot overhang, and built of white oak with walls 14 feet high.

The townspeople were assessed for its cost. The work was let on competitive bids, with the provision that the citizens help the contractor with the heavy beams. The winning contractor bid a price of 1,200 livres (about $300) in shaved deer skins. It was completed in the Spring of 1776, on Rue des L'eglise, about midway between Rue de la Tour and Rue de la Place. Just to the south of the new log church (the graveyard was on the north), he and his parishioners built a two-story residence of stone, a structure which was to last nearly a half-century.

With the arrival of the Capuchin from New Orleans, there was little need for the aged Meurin or the energetic Gibault to visit their old friends in St. Louis. In 1777, Gibault was alone; the great pioneer of the middle valley, Sebastian Meurin, was laid to rest at Prairie du Rocher. (When the Jesuits returned several decades later, his body was transferred to St. Stanislaus novitiate in Florissant.)

In 1776, the American Declaration of Independence was regarded by most of the inhabitants of the right bank as little more than an interesting development in a war definitely foreign. They were, after all, French, and Breed's Hill was still half a world away. For the first two years of that war, the British of the middle valley saw no activity of any consequence, and thus were lulled into a sense of complacency that proved disastrous to the mother country in 1778. Most of the garrison of the little stone fort at Kaskaskia had been withdrawn to counter the American and Indian thrusts in the Detroit area. The civilian population, by and large, was far from gripped with revolutionary fever, but they weren't partial to the British either. They wanted only peace.

All was quiet at the mouth of the Kaskaskia when, in the dead of the night of July 4, 1778, George Rogers Clark and his band of "Virginians" (actually Kentucky adventurers) infiltrated the garrison and demanded its surrender.

While the Long Knives greatly outnumbered the British soldiery, the tough townspeople greatly outnumbered the Virginians. The civilians requested, and were granted, permission to assemble in the church for Mass and a general discussion of the predicament.

The diplomatic Clark met first with Gibault, under the correct assumption that the priest had the unanimous respect of the townspeople in temporal as well as spiritual matters.

Gibault seconded Clark's assertions that the residents had nothing to lose by acquiescence to the American authority, that in all probability they would be far better off under the American policy of absolute freedom of worship than under the British Quebec Act of 1774. The flag of Virginia was raised, and from that moment, Clark depended heavily upon the missionary priest to accomplish his ends without bloodshed.

Gibault, at Clark's behest, rode at the head of a detachment of Long Knives as they traveled from one outpost to another, quickly dispelling the fears of the civilian population. Within 10 days all the posts in the middle valley were under military command of the State of Virginia.

Clark was aware that the British would attempt a pincer maneuver to cut his lines of communication and supplies from the east. The target of this move would have to be Vincennes, that strategic and easily-defended fort on the Wabash. Gibault had no reason to expect from those residents the same complacency as exhibited by his parishioners along the Mississippi. He offered to accompany an expedition of civilians, led by a leading citizen of Kaskaskia, a Dr. Laffont, and to attempt to enlist Vincennes on the side of the Americans.

It took the small party only a day or two to persuade the townspeople to deliver an oath of allegiance to Virginia. Thus, through the efforts of this methodical priest, the boundaries of the republic were extended to the Mississippi on the west, and the Illinois river on the north.

Clark was a man of no small vanity, and the writings he left tend to minimize—even ridicule—the role of the missionary Gibault. His actions, however, left little doubt of the high respect in which he held this man of the cloth.

The commandant of the British in Detroit had no such misgivings about Gibault—he was high on the "most wanted" list, most certainly branded with the crime of high treason. At a time when Clark had good reason to suspect that a British counterthrust might penetrate deep into Illinois country, he transported Gibault into hiding in Spanish territory.

Gibault's actions earned the displeasure of the bishop of Quebec, who dispatched a letter recalling him to the see city. It is possible that Gibault never received the letter. At any rate, he stayed where he was. When in later years Gibault asked for permission to return, it was summarily denied, causing him to live out his days in the valley he served so well.

During the last years of the revolution, Spain, like Holland, had been drawn into the war against its maritime rival, Great Britain. Thus, the settlements along the west bank of the Mississippi became attractive targets for the British. While St. Louis could mount a formidable defense against a water invasion, nothing stood between the town and an attack from the other three directions but a 15-year-old cattle fence. Don Fernando de Leyba, commandant of the Spanish garrison, had exhibited a curiously nonchalant attitude toward the danger, despite the growing apprehension on the part of the citizenry. At their own expense, the people of St. Louis began the erection of fortifications, after a plan prepared by Auguste Chouteau. They felt such emplacements would serve to protect the town against a land attack of reasonable force.

St. Louisans had abundant reason for their uneasiness. Early in 1780, the British commandant of Fort Michilimackinac was in the process of organizing an Indian expedition against St. Louis. The advance scouts of the British force reached the east bank on the festival of Corpus Christi, May 25, 1780.

After the traditional procession, which wound through the village streets, the townspeople utilized the balance of that spring Sunday to pick the first of the crop of strawberries from the commonfields.

One townsman, however, decided to angle for a few catfish near the east bank. He heard his name called. Turning toward the bank, he spotted a former acquaintance, who happened to be one of the three Frenchmen leading the attack. When he saw the brush teeming with poorly-concealed Indians, he reeled in quickly and paddled for home. De Leyba greeted his warning with disdain, reportedly locking him up for drunkenness.

The advance party of the British contingent considered an attack then and there, but decided to await the arrival of the main force the following day. They presumed the gathering of strawberries in the unprotected commonfields was an everyday occurrence—that the capture of the bulk of the inhabitants would be an elementary exercise.

The enemy flotilla crossed the river late that night, encircling the village and concealing themselves in the brush. They awaited the emergence of the townspeople on Monday morning. Only a few came out of the gates. The Indians waited with growing disappointment for more, finally attacked the few with a savage war whoop. The general commotion alerted the citizens within the walls and fortifications were manned with great dispatch.

Only a handful of unfortunates—perhaps 40 or 50—were caught outside the walls. De Leyba cowered in his stone house, and ordered his men to fill their cannon with sand. He found, however, that his men were cowering along with him, and the courageous townsmen manned the Spanish cannon themselves. The Indians fell back before the blistering fire of the fight-loving woodrangers and mountain men; the cannonade directed against them quickly nullified their bravado. The enemy was cut off from their boats in the ensuing panic. They retreated to the woods to tomahawk and scalp the small number of hapless farmers and slaves who sought refuge there.

The following is a notation in the records of The Old Cathedral:

> "On the 26th of May, 1780, I, Capuchin priest and missionary, have buried in the cemetery of this parish the bodies of Charles Bizet, Amable Guion, Calve and son, and a negro Chancelier massacred by the Indians. In the faith whereof I have signed this, the day and year as above.
>
> F. Bernard, Missionary."

With that, the war in the West drew to a virtual close, although the second Treaty of Paris was not signed until 1783. By that act, the territory of the United States was extended to the great river, and

23

the British formally recognized the independence of her former colonies.

The people of the city were furious at the cowardly conduct of the Spanish governor. De Leyba drew up his will on June 10 of that year. Two weeks later he was dead. Whether his was an act of traitorism or of cowardice will never be known.

The following two decades were years of unrest and uneasiness for those on the east side of the Mississippi. The passage of the Northwest Ordinance in 1787 elicited great apprehension on the part of the landholders, because many of them owned a number of slaves. The enforcement of the anti-slavery section would have cost them dearly. And Protestants among them had no place to go, with the Spanish crown forbidding settlement across the river to any but Roman Catholics. The lack of a clear cut delineation of ecclesiastical authority in the American Illinois proved disquieting to the clergy. Were they under the diocese of Quebec and the French, or Baltimore and the Americans? There was a vast difference, for until the French Revolution the crown had provided much of the support for the missionary priests, while of course the Congress provided nothing. This reliance on temporal support from a citizenry not used to giving it eventually led to Gibault's transfer into Spanish Louisiana.

De Leyba died on June 28, 1780, before the completion of the fort designed by Auguste Chouteau. The task of its completion fell to his successor, Don Francisco Cruzat. There was a circular stone tower, Fort San Carlos, at about Fourth and Olive Streets, four blocks north and one block west of The Old Cathedral. Another tower was erected on the site of the Poplar street bridge approach, a third between there and the river, and a square stone tower near the Eads bridge approach. A palisade of logs connected the towers. Loopholes for small arms fire were placed in the walls, and cannon were emplaced in the towers. Completion of the fort proved completely unnecessary. St. Louis was never again to be attacked. As a result the palisades rotted away and the towers gradually were removed. Hardly a trace was left by the time Du Bourg arrived in 1818.

Bernard de Limpach was witness not only to the growth of the Parish of St. Louis, but of four new settlements surrounding it on the Missouri side. On or near the site of the long gone Mission of St. Francis Xavier, near the mouth of River des Peres, a Frenchman named Clement Delor de Treget constructed a small stone house. The settlement which grew around the trader's village eventually became known as Carondelet.

The year 1786 probably saw the founding of St. Ferdinand, or Florissant, now the sixth largest city in Missouri, about 18 miles northwest of the downtown riverfront. At one time its rich black loam satisfied a large part of the agricultural needs of the metropolis to the southeast.

St. Charles became the earliest white settlement north of the Missouri river, having been founded in 1769 about 20 miles northwest of St. Louis. The village housed about 80 families by 1897.

About 25 miles north of St. Louis, on the west bank of the Mississippi, is the little town of Portage des Sioux, founded by François Saucier in 1765. Joined by a group of Creoles, he laid out the post in 1799, serving as its commandant until the end of the Spanish regime.

Limpach served them all, finally received a favorable answer to his petition for recall, and left his old parish in 1789.

There is some question whether the Dominican from Canada, Jean Antoine Ledru (Le Bru) actually served as a parish priest here, although he served the community for some years from the Illinois side.

There is no question about his successor, the celebrated Benedictine Dom Pierre Joseph Didier. At the outbreak of the French Revolution's Reign of Terror, Didier was stationed where angels feared to tread—the Abbey Church of St. Denis, place of sepulture of the French monarchs since the year 638. On July 31, 1793, the enraged mobs ravaged the church, exhumed the long-dead kings and queens and threw their bodies into lime pits.

Didier escaped to Spain, eventually ending up in St. Louis, where he became pastor in 1794. One of his early acts was to cause the erection of a large wood cross on a rather elaborate stone base, which would throw its shadow over the town for a quarter of a century. It stood just inside the walls on Olive street, about 70 yards northwest of the chapel of the towering Mansion House complex.

A period of rapid growth transpired in the next few years. The new lieutenant governor, Zenon Trudeau, came up from New Orleans. Trudeau was somewhat out of sympathy with the crippling restriction allowing only Catholics to immigrate into Spanish Louisiana. He didn't hesitate to let Illinois families know he winked at the law.

Most of the resultant growth, however, was in the farm lands and the communities to the south of St. Louis.

In 1795, the new Bishop of Louisiana, Penalver, called for a census of St. Louis. Didier replied the following year, stating that there were 1,836 residents, with no more than two dozen Protestant families, in the St. Louis area.

An earlier report by Trudeau to his governor-general indicated a growing number of non-French Catholics in the vicinity of Florissant. Complaining that there was no priest in that village, he said: "It would not be a bad thing to send them a priest of the Irish nation."

The "priest of the Irish nation"—James Maxwell—appeared shortly thereafter, not for Florissant but, of all places, the solidly French Ste. Genevieve. Yet, the 50-year-old priest was kindly received, and unsuccessfully attempted to attract an Irish colony for the west bank.

✝   ✝   ✝

The pioneers of the middle valley were subjected to hardships and inconveniences that would seem almost unsurmountable to contemporary society, but their life was idyllic compared with the ravages being perpetrated in Europe as the 19th century opened. Napolean had crushed the Italians, escaped a British noose on the Nile and defeated the Austrians. Thus, the Spanish were of no mind to quibble when the tough little Corsican demanded the return of Louisiana. Retrocession was effected in 1800 by the Treaty of St. Ildefonso. Administration of the middle valley remained with the Spanish, but the French gave the orders.

For years, regulations and taxation imposed by the French on the Mississippi river commerce had been aggravating and costly to the people on and along the river. President Thomas Jefferson concluded that the great river and its western shores must be obtained for the Union either by gold or steel—cash or war. Bonaparte, who needed cash to finance his planned war with England, proved to be a good listener. He accepted the $15,000,000 American offer for all of Louisiana on April 30, 1803. Jefferson, startled by the Union's amazing good fortune, called a special session of Congress, where the purchase was ratified on October 21, 1803. The size of the United States was more than doubled by a stroke of a pen.

✝   ✝   ✝

The Americans elected to formally divide the territory into two portions, and Major Amos Stoddard of the United States Army was appointed military governor of Upper Louisiana.

Since a Spanish commandant (Don Carlos De Hault De Lassus) still commanded the territory, the decision was made to transfer power back to France, and then to the United States. Stoddard waited at Kaskaskia from November until February, when the ice stopped running, before sending word to Don Carlos that he was ready to take possession.

Early on March 9, 1804, the Americans crossed the river from Cahokia. The column of men was led by Stoddard and the President's personal secretary, Captain Meriwether Lewis of Virginia. A fife and drum corps sounded a crisp cadence. Resplendent in their uniforms, the Spanish garrison stood at rigid attention, every eye on the column moving up the stone pathway from the boats to the government house. Don Carlos handed the keys to Major Stoddard, on behalf of the French. After a cannonade, he addressed his final message to the townspeople:

"People of Upper Louisiana, by order of the King I am now about to surrender this post and its dependencies. The flag which has protected you during nearly 36 years will no longer be seen. The oath you took now ceases to bind. Your faithfulness and courage in upholding it will be remembered forever. From the bottom of my heart I wish you all prosperity."

The column then continued ascension of the path, past the log church, to the fort on the ridge. Don Carlos wept as the Spanish flag was lowered; the Creoles burst into cheers as the banner of France was flown.

LOUISIANA A PART OF THE UNITED STATES—1804

The Spanish troops then left the fort to sail to New Orleans, tugging at their antiquated cannons and other munitions of defense. The Americans inspected their new quarters.

When Stoddard sent for the French flag at sunset, the Creoles sent up such a cry that he felt it prudent to leave the banner aloft all night, watched by a volunteer guard of honor. The town, evidently, went wild. Frenchmen reminisced of their early years in the provinces and the splendor of the regal processions. A singer led ballads of the Old Country. But they were yearning for a France of Louis XIV, a France that was no more.

Early on the morning of March 10, 1804, the French ensign was lowered to the accompaniment of a funereal roll. Then the Stars and Stripes burst in the breeze, the fife and drum corps struck into lively music. Charles Gratiot, a Swiss, reportedly cried, "Three cheers for the American flag!" His exhortation fell on deaf ears. There were no cheers. The era of France in North America had passed, never to return.

Pierre Janin, secular priest who had been pastor of the parish of St. Louis since the departure of Didier, did not feel up to maintaining his church under the American flag, and set out for New Orleans in November, 1804. The parish was left without an accredited pastor until Du Bourg's arrival, some 14 years later.

✝   ✝   ✝

Now that President Jefferson had won the vast territory of Louisiana for the young nation, it logically followed that more information on its resources and routes of navigation was needed. He ordered his secretary, Lewis, to assemble an expedition to penetrate it to the Pacific Ocean.

He selected as his co-leader William Clark, younger brother of the Revolutionary War hero, who was destined to become governor of the Missouri territory. Shortly after the transfer, the expedition departed from Wood River and headed up the wide Missouri. They came upon the Columbia river and followed it to its mouth. The explorers returned to St. Louis September 23, 1806, with a large measure of the information sought by the President. The adventure is important to this narrative because practically all of the territory through which they passed was to become, in 20 years, part of the diocese of St. Louis.

✝   ✝   ✝

St. Louis was served, from 1806 to 1808, by a controversial Capuchin named Thomas Flynn. His ministrations to the community and its dependencies were strictly by contract. No records are available to establish his official appointment as pastor by a higher authority. It is presumed he was pastor without portfolio. He resigned January 8, 1808, and no further information on his later whereabouts has come to light. Maxwell continued to make regular journeys to St. Louis throughout the years.

Chapter IV

DU BOURG—THE ARTFUL PERSUADER

In 1801, the Bishop of Louisiana left New Orleans for an Archbishopric in Guatemala. A new bishop, approved by Pius VII and consecrated in Spain, never arrived—the retrocession and subsequent sale of the territory prompted him to accept a Spanish diocese instead. Thus, the entire territory was left without a Bishop.

John Carroll, Bishop of Baltimore, feeling this situation was not in the best interest of the thousands of Catholics in the valley, assumed guardianship of the territory "until the Holy See provided otherwise." Jean Olivier was appointed vicar general.

The pastor of the cathedral in New Orleans, the Capuchin Antonio de Sedella, flatly refused to recognize Carroll's right to make any such appointment. Sedella is generally described as a cantankerous and troublesome person, who probably aspired to the purple himself. Carroll felt it necessary to appeal to Rome.

Because of the wars on the continent, it wasn't until 1808 that an answer was received. Carroll was given Papal authority to appoint an administrator for the Louisiana territory.

Carroll searched his records for a man to fill the post. He had to serve a vast, multi-lingual area. He had to have administrative and executive experience. Obviously he wouldn't find such a man in the west. He found him near Baltimore, the distinguished Sulpician educator and former president of Georgetown University, Louis William Du Bourg. He was appointed Apostolic Administrator in 1812.

✝   ✝   ✝

Du Bourg was born on Cap François on the island of Santo Domingo on February 4, 1766. His family moved to Bordeaux two years later. Like many of the priests who emigrated to the New World, Du Bourg was forced to leave the France of the revolution.  In 1792 he fled from the College of Issy, where he held a professorship, disguised as a minstrel with a fiddle under his arm. In 1794 he left Spain for Baltimore, where he was admitted into the Sulpician community. He became president of Georgetown in 1796. In 1799 he founded the Seminary of St. Mary's in Baltimore. Fortunately for St. Louis, Du Bourg was not a fighting man. This was soon to be proved by the jealous and aggravating Sedella of New Orleans.

LOUIS WILLIAM DU BOURG

Du Bourg left for New Orleans on October 18, 1812. For a period of three years Sedella yielded to the authority of the new Administrator. Du Bourg's problems mounted, and by 1815 he found his normal complement of 14 priests reduced by half. Four died within an 18-month period and three were old and infirm. Whatever Du Bourg lacked in firmness was more than compensated by his ability to establish persuasive rapport with the highest powers of the continent, both ecclesiastical and temporal. In 1815, therefore, he announced his intention to personally level an appeal for help to the Vatican. He appointed Louis Sibourd as his Vicar General, to serve with Du Bourg's authority until the latter's return. The wrath of Sedella, smouldering a thousand days, burst again in open rebellion. Du Bourg patiently documented his authority for unseeing eyes, then left the problem in Sibourd's lap. By a letter dispatched to Rome from France, Du Bourg succeeded in getting the Vatican to demand Sedella's obedience to authority, and again the fiery Capuchin was subdued.

In the process of his face-to-face appeal to Pius VII, Du Bourg not only won the promise of immediate and meaningful help, but the appointment as Bishop of Louisiana as well. He was consecrated in Rome September 24, 1815.

The intensity of politics in contemporary American government rivals the elaborate moves of Du Bourg on the continent. While in Rome he had the good fortune to be quartered in the mother house of the Congregation of the Mission. There he was captivated with the personality and potential administrative ability of the young teaching priest, Felix de Andreis. The superior of the mother house, Charles Dominic Sicardi, also was quite aware of the abilities of de Andreis, and Du Bourg's entreaties evoked only the greatest of Sicardi's sympathies. After all, he, Sicardi, had seen him first. But Du Bourg wanted this man to head his seminary, which he hoped would be a fountainhead of local-born priests to serve his Louisiana. He knew his political power in Rome, and he resolved to test it. The powerful Papal Secretary of State, Ercole Cardinal Consalvi, was enlisted on the side of Du Bourg. To make sure his maneuver could not abort, he then sought and obtained the backing of Pius VII himself to the cause. The poor Lazarist capitulated, probably wishing he had some quiet little parish in the country. On September 27, 1815, Felix de Andreis was assigned to the great diocese beyond the Mississippi.

Back home, old Father Maxwell, off on one of his interminable missionary journeys, was killed in a fall from his horse. He was buried in the church at Ste. Genevieve, where his body rests to this day. Young Henri Pratte, son of one of Maxwell's parishioners, was ordained at the seminary in Quebec. The bishop of Bardstown, Kentucky, acting in the absence of Du Bourg, appointed Pratte to succeed Maxwell in his home town. Thus, at the age of 27, he became the first "home grown" priest in Missouri. He was to become a tower of strength and an unexpected bonus for Du Bourg, and his name is written large in the history of Ste. Genevieve. He is now interred beside Maxwell.

✝   ✝   ✝

FELIX DE ANDREIS

De Andreis lost no time in justifying Du Bourg's enthusiasm over his abilities. The pair stormed Europe, obtaining men and money for the diocese. DeAndreis' first recruit was one of his pupils in the mother house, Joseph Rosati, who had undertaken the study of English. The two of them convinced several others to join in the great adventure. On October 14, not three weeks after the appointment of De Andreis, Rosati led the little band from Rome to Marseilles. De Andreis remained several weeks longer to obtain books, religious articles and more money for the Louisiana churches.

Picking up several more priests and a few seminarians, the De Andreis contingent joined Rosati's group in Toulouse, then proceeded to Bordeaux to await the arrival of Du Bourg.

Du Bourg, too, continued his missionary efforts, and persuaded a number of priests to join him. He executed one of the most important coups of his career when, at Lyons, he succeeded in ingratiating himself with Madame Petit, who at the time was involved with the organization of a group which would become known as the Society for the Propagation of the Faith. It was this organization which soon would be called upon to save the infant diocese of St. Louis from insolvency.

Reports from New Orleans were so grim and foreboding, resulting from the maneuvering of the diabolical Sedella, that Du Bourg began to think of another location for his cathedral. In a letter to Cardinal Dugnani he said, "My friends entertain fears about my personal safety, should I appear in the city."

He suggested that his home city might well be St. Louis, and noted that his appearances in New Orleans would be few and far between, "since it is almost entirely under the influence of that wretched Religious."

Presuming an affirmative answer to his proposal from the Vatican, Du Bourg informed De Andreis of his plans. The young priest and all his growing band accepted the change with high enthusiasm, most of them intensifying their study of English, since the use of French was diminishing in Upper Louisiana.

It had been a full seven months since the little group at Bordeaux had seen their bishop, and a few of them, growing discouraged, returned to Rome. But Du Bourg arrived in Bordeaux May 22, 1816, with new volunteers to take their places. With De Andreis in charge, they embarked two weeks later on the American brigantine *Ranger*. There was only one other passenger aboard, a Quaker, who must have found it a little disconcerting to have been so greatly outnumbered. The weather during the crossing was so tempestuous that the non-Catholic captain repeatedly called upon the priests and seminarians to re-double their prayers. After six weeks afloat, the *Ranger* dropped anchor in Baltimore harbor on July 26, 1816.

Before hearing from the Vatican on his proposed change of the see city from New Orleans to St. Louis, Du Bourg had asked the opinion of his old friend, Benedict Joseph Flaget, Bishop of Bardstown. Flaget spent seven months investigating the settlements along the Mississippi and the Missouri, and was greatly surprised to find "upwards of 10,000 Catholics in residence" there, with more conversions pouring in constantly.

Although he didn't disagree with Du Bourg's suggestion, he did go on record as being extremely disappointed in the state of "extreme indifference" in which the inhabitants of St. Louis regarded their religion. He noted that the parishioners had contracted with Francis Savine, of Cahokia, for services every third Sunday. Aside from this, they were without priestly ministrations except in case of emergency.

The Bishop capitalized upon the outside chance that the honored town might be Ste. Genevieve by imposing some pre-Victorian sentiments upon the people of St. Louis. In a letter advising the citizens that theirs might be the see city, he pointed out the manifold advantages of such an eventuality and advised an early start on planning for the temporal sustenance of the contingent from Rome. He went on: "As the location of the see will mainly depend on the recommendation which, we, Msgr. Du Bourg and myself, will make, I am determined to oppose with all my power, the selection of St. Louis; if it be true, what has been written to me, that a theatre was opened there, which must neutralize the efforts of even the most zealous and most Holy Bishop."

"Indeed," he adds, "what would it profit a prelate to inveigh ever so earnestly against the vanities, luxuries and intrigues, when the play-actors may preach in principle and in practice, the intrigues, the luxuries and vanities of the world? That would mean to mingle light with darkness, truth with falsehood, Belial with the God of Israel."

Following a tradition that endures to this day in St. Louis, the theatre evidently went broke, for within a few months Flaget was to advise the Bishop of Baltimore that a St. Louis location was "of the utmost importance for the good of religion."

THE VILLAGE OF ST. LOUIS IN 1770. FIRST (SPANISH) CHURCH IS ABOVE LARGE
CHOUTEAU HOME IN CENTER OF PICTURE.

The St. Louis of 1816 still had a population of only 2,000—French, Creole, English, Negroes, and a few Indians, still fewer Irish. The fur trade still was the principal occupation, as the industrial revolution still was many years from St. Louis. The best skilled workmen made wages of $2 to $3 a day, a rather handsome sum in those days. The steamboat was just around the bend; the first and forerunner of the mighty commerce of mid-century would arrive in 1817. Tobacco was in such demand as to be placed under cultivation. Duels limited the dockets of the Civil Courts, and Bloody Island (long since wedded to East St. Louis) came by its name honestly. It was the land of the rolling bones and the one-eyed Jack. Chance was king and Lady Luck was queen. Du Bourg and his men would not want for things to do.

De Andreis, Rosati and their companions couldn't enjoy an extended stay in the city of Baltimore, as they wished to cross the Alleghenies before the Fall rains made the mud roads impassable. Eight of them set out for Bardstown by stage. But the rains came early that year. At a place called Bloody Run, the caravan was detained for three days by constant rain, after which the driver advised them he would go no further. De Andreis procured a wagon for their baggage, and the party set out for Pittsburgh on foot. Rome was beginning to look mighty good.

After a five-week stay in Pittsburgh, awaiting the rains on the west slope which would make the river navigable, the band proceeded down the Ohio in a flatboat, arriving in Louisville November 19, 1816.

Flaget had made a number of trips to Louisville in anticipation of their arrival, but, as it happened, when they did arrive he was back in Bardstown. By letter, he urged them to winter in his seminary rather than proceed to the town of St. Louis, which had not at that time made provision for their housing. Besides, all of them could use the educational facilities to advance their studies of English and French.

In the Spring of 1816, after bidding his recruits *bon voyage*, Du Bourg continued his mission of rounding up men, money and materials for Louisiana. He advised the Vatican that he had no intention of coming to St. Louis until he received assurance that Sedella's poison had not been wafted upriver. As winter approached, Rome grew uneasy and asked what, if anything, was going on. Du

Bourg replied that much had taken place, and indeed it had. A second contingent, this one composed of postulants for the Ursuline convent, had sailed for New Orleans.

The fact was they very nearly returned to Paris. When the superior of their convent heard about the antics of Sedella, she petitioned Pius VII to allow their recall to Paris, fearing the loyalty of the nuns to Du Bourg would prompt Sedella to deny them the sacraments. The Pope assured her the authority of the bishop would be obeyed. Nine of the young ladies reached their new home January 3. 1817.

Du Bourg, by that time, also had recruited a dozen more volunteers for America. He received from Mother Barat, now Saint Madeleine Sophia, the promise of a colony of the Ladies of the Sacred Heart.

A year later, a group of four of the nuns left for St. Louis. Heading them was the now-beatified 47-year-old Mother Philippine Duchesne.

Titled families in France and the low countries gave him money, vestments, and books. Some of the paintings garnered by the hard driving prelate still hang in The Old Cathedral; others were given to the cathedral at Bardstown, still more to the cathedral of New Orleans.

✝   ✝   ✝

De Andreis did not allow the impatience of his group to turn to boredom. He soon had them hard at work in the little log house known as the seminary. Aside from the study of the languages of the frontier, there was little semblance to formal education. The soft Italians soon were spending half their waking hours astraddle a horse, visiting isolated bands of Catholics in the Ohio country. Their insides, too, were toughened by the frontier fare, "cornbread badly baked, tough salt pork, potatoes and water." While the frail De Andreis crammed for a working knowledge of the Indian dialects of the Trans-Mississippi, the adventure-loving Rosati preached to the far-flung Kentucky woodsmen. They were used to seeing their priests in buckskins—Rosati brought them in from miles around to see the "Roman priest dressed like a woman."

Chapter V

DU BOURG—AT THE FRONTIER

Louis XVIII, the Citizen King, provided the frigate *La Caravane* for Du Bourg's party, which sailed for America July 1, 1817. By now, Du Bourg had 29 in his group, most of which decided to practice their apostolic efforts on the ship's crew. During the two months at sea, Du Bourg confirmed 35 officers and men. The frigate docked at Annapolis September 4, 1817. Some days later she set sail again for Europe and was never heard from again. She went down in a hurricane with all hands.

Du Bourg, still uneasy over the possibility of Sedella's influence in the middle valley, wrote Flaget from St. Mary's asking him to proceed to St. Louis to determine the general attitude of the townspeople, and to find out if they were willing to raise the funds necessary to erect a cathedral, support the contingent of clergy, and reimburse the party for their expenses in traveling from Baltimore to St. Louis. Although Flaget was under no obligation to honor the request, he set out immediately on the 300-mile journey, together with De Andreis, Rosati, and a Brother Blanca.

Nine days later they arrived at Kaskaskia. After a few days of rest, they were joined by Donatien Olivier on the upstream voyage to Ste. Genevieve. It was there that the party first met young Henri Pratte. Two days later, on October 17, the group was in St. Louis, but not even their fatigue could dull the bitterness of their disappointment at what they found.

Rosati describes their arrival: "The Bishop and the missionaries went to the presbytery, which was an old stone building almost in ruins, divided by planks into two portions, one of which, the smaller of the two, served as a sleeping room, and the other was apportioned to ... assemblies. In this tottering house Bishop Flaget determined to take up his residence, and as there was no bed in it, some of the inhabitants prepared one for him. Father de Andreis and his companions had to sleep on buffalo skins spread on the floor, in the same room or the adjoining ... The parish church, situated very near the presbytery, was in no better condition. It was small, poor and falling into ruins. In a word, wherever the eye turned, nothing could be seen but poverty and desolation."

BENEDICT FLAGET, BISHOP OF BARDSTOWN

Flaget immediately assembled the leading citizens of the small community, driving home the fiscal as well as spiritual values of having a bishop in their midst, emphasizing that this would attract much growth to the town, and greatly increase land values. He cited as the first order of business the erection of a suitable episcopal residence.

There were some objections to the entreaties, but the great body of citizens endorsed the need. The Irishman Jeremiah Connor touched things off with an offer of $1,000.

There weren't many Protestants in the little town, but some of them displayed an unusual spirit of ecumenicity. Among the non-Catholic givers was Thomas Hart Benton, destined to become Missouri's first Senator.

Flaget soon left for Bardstown, leaving Henri Pratte to return the church and rectory to a usable condition until new facilities could be built. De Andreis took his place in Ste. Genevieve. In Bardstown, Rosati assumed charge of the seminary and awaited the arrival of Du Bourg.

Softened by the hospitality of Europe for the past three years, Du Bourg had even a worse time with the Alleghenies than his advance party. He writes from Pittsburgh on November 13, 1817:

"What roads! What precipices! What break necks! I do not remember having endured, in my life, such fatigue. After walking half of the second day to avoid dislocating our limbs, on the third we could not escape the overturn of the stage which, that very day, was upset three times. When the first accident took place we were all in the carriage, at the moment of the second, it was empty, and when it was overthrown the third time, all were in except Augustin, Mr. Blanc and myself. We had bravely made up our minds to foot the road. All our fellow-travelers at last took the same resolution. We happily executed our resolution, but not without incredible trouble. The third evening especially we were obliged, for the security of our luggage which had already been upset twice, to follow the stage more than three hours after sunset. Without a ray of light to guide us, we constantly fell into mud and water. When not in sloppy plains, we had to walk over slippery rocks which hurt our feet, while wild briars scratched our faces."

The party boarded a flatboat and floated down the Ohio, arriving at Bardstown December 2. On December 18, the two prelates left on the steamer *Piqua* for St. Louis, in hopes of arriving before Christmas. The passenger list included, according to Flaget, "seven or eight comedians, a like number of Jews, the band of four Religious, besides others, both black and white . . . (The boat) might serve successively for a synagogue, a cathedral, a theatre, a hospital, a parlor, a dining room and a sleeping apartment. It is in fact a veritable Noah's Ark . . . and what is more astonishing, peace and harmony reign here."

Huge ice floes confined the craft to the middle of the river, where it was stuck for two days. They arose Christmas morning at the mouth of the Ohio, precisely where they had been Christmas eve. She took on some more wood at the mouth of Apple Creek. On New Year's Eve, Du Bourg and De Andreis were united at Ste. Genevieve. On January 4th they spent the evening with Savine at Cahokia.

Early on the morning of January 5, 1818, a contingent of 40 mounted Cahokians escorted the episcopal party to a small boat on the Illinois levee. As the group neared the Missouri shore, they could see a great gathering—nearly all of the townspeople of St. Louis, Catholic and Protestant alike. There was a tumultuous cheer as the line was caught on the Missouri shore and the great prelate ended his three-year journey.

Both Bishops led the cheering procession up the stone walk to the rectory, where they changed into their full pontifical vestments. They were received by four prominent parishioners bearing a silken canopy. Preceded by 12 altar boys, Flaget led Du Bourg to the episcopal throne, fashioned so recently by Henri Pratte in the little log church of 1776.

Flaget's message of introduction was so moving that whatever remained of the pestilential blast from New Orleans was forever removed in a few brief moments. Two days later, the selfless Flaget went back to his work in Bardstown. Du Bourg's tears of gratitude were soon to change to tears of vexatious frustration.

✝   ✝   ✝

The St. Louis of Du Bourg's day still was a town of about 2,000 whites and 400 or 500 Negroes, of which practically all were at least nominal Catholics. The First Presbyterian Church was organized in 1817 with nine members. The First Baptist Church was organized in the same year with 11 members, including two ministers.

✝   ✝   ✝

Two days after his arrival, Du Bourg's elation at his reception had waned enough for him to lend some analysis to the situation. He writes: "My cathedral, which looks like a poor stable, is falling in ruins, so that a new church is an absolute necessity."

Since Flaget had already broken the ice, Du Bourg felt he could proceed immediately with plans for his new cathedral. On March 29, 1818, he laid the cornerstone of a building which was to measure a rather awkward 135' x 40'. The brick walls were 15' high. Still uncompleted (indeed, it never was completed), it was blessed January 9, 1820.

DU BOURG'S CATHEDRAL–1820.

Du Bourg has gone down in history as something of a dreamer in the field of finance. However, in those days the temporal affairs of the church were conducted almost entirely by Marguilliers—a group of wardens elected by the congregation to collect the money necessary to keep the church in repair, pay the wages and salaries of the pastors and their assistants, and cover their expenses. The blame for whatever fiscal difficulties the church might have been in fell largely on their shoulders.

The first subscription, energized by Flaget, yielded $4,271.75—from Auguste Chouteau, $400; Pierre Chouteau, $200; A. P. Chouteau, $50;

40

Thomas Brady, $200; Jeremiah Connor, $200; Bernard Pratte, $300; John B. Sarpy, $20; Alexander McNair, $100; B. Berthold, $100; John Mullanphy, $100; Theodore Papin, $20; Theodore Hunt, $100; Frederick Bates, $100; Thomas H. Benton, $100 (added $50 later); M. Sanguinet, $50; Henry Von Puhl, $50 (paid $30); Francis Robidoux, $60 (paid $30); William Carr, $100 (paid $50); P. B. and J. P. B. Gratiot, $30 (paid $50); Anthony Soulard, $50; J. P. Cabanne, $20; Wm. Clark, $100 (paid $75); and Manuel Lisa, $150.

A second subscription netted $1,303.36, some months later. The sale of materials in the old church brought $110. The pews in the new church were offered for sale, bringing $6,786.38. Altogether, a total of $15,500 of the necessary $20,000 was raised, through a diversity of sources.

Generally depressed business conditions during the "Panic of 1819" precluded raising any more money from the people of the little town, so Auguste and Pierre Chouteau, with Bernard Pratte, made themselves personally responsible for the remaining $4,500.

✝   ✝   ✝

Simultaneous with the building of the church, Du Bourg ordered the start of a college—one which was the forerunner of the great St. Louis University of today. It replaced the two-room accommodation in the home of Mme. Alvarez, where classes had begun in 1818. Francis Niel, a young man ordained to the priesthood by Du Bourg in the log church just two months after his arrival, was placed in charge of the building program. Niel evidently put up the building funds himself.

The structure was built of brick, two stories high, just to the east of the present Old Cathedral, facing Walnut street. It also served as a rectory for the bishop and his staff.

Its life as a college was just nine years—Du Bourg was forced to close it because of lack of teaching priests necessitated hiring lay instructors at a total cost exceeding the school's income. It later served as a chapel seating 600 persons, and as a free school for boys from 1844 until it was destroyed by the great fire of 1849.

The Chouteaus and Pratte, victims of a lingering business depression, petitioned the territorial legislature for, and won, authority to offer the south half of the church block for sale to satisfy their note for $4,500. This included the ground on which the Old Cathedral stands today. At the subsequent auction, Niel was the only bidder —for $1,205. He then transferred the title to all the ground except the college plot to the three wardens, in partial satisfaction of the indebtedness. It was not to be until 1832, long after the partition of the Louisiana diocese and Rosati's appointment as Bishop, that the three patient men were repaid in full.

All of the north half of the church lot not occupied by the Spanish church of 1770 was designated for cemetery use, but in 1823 the Trustees of St. Louis passed legislation prohibiting burials within the city limits of that day. It became an additional burden of the hard-pressed parishioners to pay for the removal of the 2,000 dead to a new tract on the St. Charles road, about a mile northwest of the city limits. The transfer was effected in 1831.

When it became the lot of De Andreis to accompany his Bishop to St. Louis in 1818, the responsibility of establishing a permanent seminary in Upper Louisiana fell to his pupil, Joseph Rosati. It was placed near Perryville, some 80 miles southeast of St. Louis, and called "The Barrens," after their old home on the salt barrens of Kentucky. The bishop had levied the people of the surrounding area heavily—the sum of $7,500—for its construction. Some 23 priests, seminarians and brothers arrived in the area in October, 1818, immediately set to work completing the main seminary building. From this structure and its successors, St. Mary's of the Barrens supplied a steady stream of priests to the diocese. It is still in existence, still performing its original function. The new building received the earthly remains of De Andreis, who died in St. Louis October 15, 1820.

Du Bourg never could be called a master politician. When things were going well for him, he had the faculty of compounding his successes. In the face of political adversity, he was a failure. He often made decisions without mature deliberation, and without consulting his trusted subordinates, whose advice could have kept him from error. He was destined to make two errors of such magnitude that they would serve to drive him from his American episcopate eight short years after his arrival in St. Louis.

Long before Du Bourg's arrival in St. Louis, there was talk of the partition of the northern and southern portions of Louisiana into two separate dioceses. Du Bourg, however, felt the time was not right, electing rather to appoint, with the approval of Rome, a coadjutor who would share with him the burdens of administration.

The news from the South brought surprising tidings of the crafty Sedella's obeisance to Du Bourg. The fight, to Du Bourg, seemed to be over. In truth, Sedella realized that he could at that time gain more with honey than vinegar. Du Bourg, in his naïveté, took the bait. In 1819, he recommended that the Vatican approve his selection of the aging Sedella as his coadjutor, with Joseph Rosati holding the actual right of succession.

Sedella had the opportunity to further ingratiate himself when, in 1820, Du Bourg paid his first episcopal visit to the city. "All manifested in unison their obedience to me and their zeal for the maintenance of ecclesiastical discipline." And the word circulated around New Orleans of the bishop's petition to Rome.

Du Bourg, however, soon had cause to change his mind, and recommended to the Vatican that they find against his original petition, on the grounds of the advanced age of the Capuchin, without, of course, revealing Du Bourg's true reason for the rejection. In recommending Rosati for the job, he urged the Vatican to take no action for a few years, until Rosati gained more experience. While the first action shocked and infuriated the many priests who knew Sedella for what he was, the second left them with a sense of disbelief. Rosati, their choice all along, was in their opinion far more qualified for the job than was the Bishop himself.

In June, 1819, Du Bourg vacillated again, this time recommending the same Louis Sibourd who was left in charge of the diocese while Du Bourg was in Europe. No doubt Rome frowned on this also, because of Sibourd's age.

A young and supposedly "titled" emigré to the diocese, Anthony Inglesi, persuaded the gullible Du Bourg to ordain him after a brief refresher course, since he claimed to have completed the curriculum at the seminary in Quebec. In 1821 Du Bourg recommended him to Rome, contingent upon his gaining some experience. Two months after his ordination he was sent to Rome to recruit more priests and seminarians.

Although Inglesi did succeed in sending a band of recruits to the New World, and although, during the course of his mission, he is credited with gathering (and embezzling) vast sums for St. Louis, the Vatican returned a report of his "scandalous" extracurricular activities in the Roman night spots. Inglesi, exposed as a complete fraud, later returned to America, became involved in a scandal and left the church. Du Bourg was reminded sternly by Rome that he broke the church's regulations by ordaining a person who had not been in his charge the minimum length of time.

So warm was Du Bourg's reception on his episcopal visit to New Orleans that he elected to make it the see city of his diocese, which included the entire Louisiana Purchase, Florida, Alabama and Mississippi, and informally, the western halves of Illinois and Wisconsin. It is reported that, while his relations with Sedella were warm, the trustees cooled to him to such an extent that at one time they told him to take his episcopal throne out of "their" Cathedral.

Du Bourg's relationships with the parishioners, too, were disintegrating rapidly. In 1823, Mrs. Charles Smith, a wealthy widow, whom the bishop had rebuffed earlier, expressed the intention of deeding her sizeable estate at Grand Coteau to the congregation. It consisted of "excellent and extensive lands, some 30 slaves, a goodly number of cattle, agricultural implements, a house, furniture, etc." Her only condition was that the congregation return to her 1/10 of the proceeds from the sale of the crops, as a living allowance. The Bishop attached so many conditions to the offer that Mrs. Smith withdrew it entirely.

The Inglesi affair left Du Bourg estranged with many of his priests. When first hearing of his desire to appoint him to the coadjutorship, several of them sent a polite letter beseeching him to reconsider. The prelate immediately issued an intemperate circular letter, for which he apologized some days later.

His relationship with Rosati must have suffered too, with his adamant insistence that the Seminary at The Barrens be moved to Lower Louisiana. Only the intervention of his old friend, Flaget, prevented the move.

In 1825, a Reverend Segura arrived in New Orleans in search of a parish. Since he bore no credentials, Du Bourg wisely refused him faculties. Segura, however, went to the parish of St. Charles of the Germans and ingratiated himself with the trustees there. They petitioned for his appointment, and again the Bishop refused, advising them that he would, however, send a qualified priest. Segura, meanwhile, took up his residence there, and the church wardens led a drive which resulted in almost daily villification of the prelate in the area newspapers.

Du Bourg, in 1826, announced to Rosati that he was going to Rome to mend some fences with church authorities, and probably to let things cool off a bit. His actual intention, however, was to resign. On November 4, Rosati received the Pontifical brief informing him of the partition of Louisiana and of his appointment as Bishop of the Diocese of New Orleans. Rosati's objections were so well-founded that the Vatican amended the edict to make Rosati bishop of St. Louis.

Du Bourg, then a broken man, sought retirement in Europe. Instead he was appointed bishop of Montauban, then archbishop of Besançon, France, where he died December 12, 1833. The New Orleans diocese, when left by Du Bourg, was in debt by 40,000 francs.

Chapter VI

ROSATI–THE CATHEDRAL BUILDER

Despite all the episcopal vacillation, Rosati was named Du Bourg's coadjutor, on March 25, 1824. He was appointed to the see of St. Louis May 20, 1827, but continued his administration of the diocese of New Orleans until Leo De Neckere was consecrated June 24, 1830.

JOSEPH ROSATI

Rosati spent the greater part of 1827 in New Orleans, and the early part of 1828 visiting the various parishes in Lower Louisiana. Early in that year an incident transpired which served to inform the laity of New Orleans that there was, indeed, a new man in charge.

A petition had been circulated asking the State Legislature for a law which would allow the Marguilliers of any parish the authority to refuse any pastors in whose appointment they did not concur. Rosati held a brief meeting with Sedella and several other ecclesiastical leaders, wherein the measure was soundly denounced.

The Bishop had no intention of stopping there. He personally set out to see a number of State Senators to show them where such a law would be in opposition to the laws of the Catholic Church, and, therefore, would be in conflict with the Constitution of the United States. The petition died aborning. There were to be no further power plays during the Rosati episcopate.

✝   ✝   ✝

Shortly after Rosati's return to St. Louis, a townsman, John Mullanphy, offered land to the diocese for use as a hospital, plus two houses, the rent from which would produce $3000 a year, plus $150 in traveling expenses of persons who could be induced to run a hospital. He also offered another lot and $350 for furnishings. On June 23, 1828, Rosati relayed the offer to the mother house of the Daughters of Charity, in Emmetsburg, Maryland. On August 28, he received a favorable answer. Four of the revered order were on their way.

Mullanphy Hospital, at Fourth and Spruce streets, was placed in operation on November 26, 1828—the first west of the Mississippi River. In October, 1832, the city was hit by an epidemic of Asiatic Cholera. The city's temporary resources were woefully inadequate, and the Sisters opened their doors to all. There were eight at the time. By the time the epidemic subsided, three weeks later, there were only six. The undaunted mother house sent three more to take their places.

In 1834, the Bishop gave to the Community a small house on the church block, between Market and Walnut on Third Street. Soon the first Catholic orphans' home of the West was open, staffed by six Daughters of Charity.

✝   ✝   ✝

By 1830, Du Bourg's old brick church was a wreck. It should have lasted longer, but the construction was even worse than the design. In an appeal to Rome, Rosati described it thusly: "It was never finished and the interior remained rustic, and looked like a barn. The work was badly done, so that a side wall 130 feet long is about to collapse . . . this Church could not serve much longer because it is dangerous to leave it in its present state and because it cannot be repaired for a sum smaller than it would take to erect a new Church. In the meanwhile, we celebrate the holy mysteries in this barn, which is about to fall, is open to rain, snow and wind. In winter, and the winters in these parts are rigorous, we cannot pass an hour at the altar without freezing . . . and often the sacred ceremonies are disturbed by the rain which the storm carries to the very steps of the altar. I have applied everywhere, I sacrificed what I could, but if the Lord does not open to us some way, we have to do without a Church."

Rosati's compelling appeals to Europe were not without result, and a standing committee on solicitations worked effectively with the citizens. Leasing the north half of the Church block provided additional cash, and Rosati held some personal funds and real estate in reserve.

It was April, 1830, when the decision was made to build a new Cathedral. On August 15 of that same year, the standing committee reported "that the walls should be three feet thick from the foundations to the floor, and two and a half above the floor; the foundation should be sunk four feet in the ground and raised five above the ground; that the church should be eighty by one hundred and thirty, and thirty-four feet high from the floor; that the front should be of neat hammered stone, and the sides of good range work."

Rosati wasn't inclined to repeat any of Du Bourg's mistakes. He wanted a church that would stand a century or more (it has); and he wanted to pay for it as it was being erected (he couldn't).

Work had progressed so far that the cornerstone laying ceremony was held on August 1, 1831.

In December, 1832, Rosati wrote to Du Bourg: "We shall not be able to finish the church for less than $18,000 more, for I reckon it will cost $30,000; but it will be built for centuries."

(Rosati probably was not computing the total completed costs— these amounted to $63,360.85.)

Late in 1834, near the close of the building period, the bishop's finances were in rugged shape. "I have borrowed more than $12,000; I have for this mortgaged all the properties which are under my name . . . should worse come . . . the sale of the mortgaged properties will yield more than is required to pay to the creditors both interest and principal; this is why I have had no scruple to go into debt, as there is no danger of any injustice to them."

✟   ✟   ✟

SKETCH OF INTERIOR OF THE OLD CATHEDRAL BY INTERIOR DECORATOR,
LEON POMEREDE.
Collection of Stratford Lee Morton

48

On October 26, 1834, Rosati consecrated the new Cathedral. The full text of Rosati's report to Pope Gregory XVI, who was one of the principal contributors to the building fund, is reproduced here, annotated with footnotes by the author.

AN ACCOUNT
OF THE CONSECRATION OF THE
NEW CATHEDRAL OF ST. LOUIS, MO.,
Celebrated on October 26, 1834
I. Description of the Church

This august temple, raised in the City of St. Louis, Mo., was begun about three years ago. The first stone thereof was blessed and set in place with the customary ceremonies on August 1st, 1831, by the present Bishop of the Diocese. Thanks to the munificence of the reigning Sovereign Pontiff, Gregory XVI, through the generous aid given by the Association for the Propagation of the Faith established in France, and of the Leopoldine Institution established in the dominions of His Majesty the Emperor of Austria; by means of the repeated efforts of the inhabitants of St. Louis who have contributed according to their capacity, either by subscriptions, or by collections taken a number of times for this purpose; finally owing to other resources drawn from a piece of property adjacent to the old church, and loans of various sums of money obtained at reasonable rates, this edifice has been continued without other interruptions than those which were caused by the rigor of the winter, which in this country does not permit building operations; and has at length been put in condition of being consecrated.

The dimensions of the church are as follows: length, 136 feet; width, 84 feet; and height, 40 feet. The entire facade, as also 27 feet of the sides near the facade, are of beautiful polished stone, much like marble.[1] The portico is sustained in front by four columns of the same material 27 feet high, and of a diameter of four feet. It is 40 feet long and 12 feet deep, Doric, after the fashion of the ruins of Paestum. On the frieze of that portico and of the whole facade is read in relief the following inscription: *In honorem* St. Ludovici. DEO UNI ET TRINO DICATUM. A. MDCCCXXXIV.[2] Above the three doors are placed three slabs of Italian marble, upon which is engraved the following text of the Apocalypse: *Ecce Tabernaculum Dei cum hominibus, et habitabit cum eis,*[3] this inscription is in Latin over the middle door, in English over the door to the east, and in French over the other. The Gospel text; *Domus mea Domus orationis vocabitur,*[4] is inscribed on two other slabs in French and in English on

---

1. Actually sandstone, which has been subject to a great deal of erosion, particularly the upper reaches of the columns. Architectural authorities, however, feel it will be another century or two before replacement will be necessary.
2. "In honor of St. Louis. Dedicated to the One and Triune God. 1834 A.D."
3. "Behold the tabernacle of God with men, and He will dwell with them."
4. "My house will be called a house of prayer."

either side of the facade. Over the parapet surmounting the outer cornice of the facade are placed six candelabra of stone.[5] The portico is crowned by a beautiful pediment in the center of which is engraved in large gilded Hebrew characters the ineffable Name of God surmounted by rays. Back of that pediment arises the belfrey, about 20 feet square and 40 feet high above the apex of the facade which itself is 50 feet high; it is all constructed of polished stone, ornamented with two rows of pilasters and cornices. In the center of the lower row of pilasters is on the four sides a clock's dial face; and in the center of the upper row are the openings of the bell-house. Time has not permitted to finish the octagonal spire, 45 feet high, before the consecration of the church, the approach of winter having compelled the workmen to suspend work until next spring. The skeleton of this spire is of wood; it will be covered outside with sheets of tin, and surmounted by a ball of gilded brass, on the top of which will be raised a cross ten feet high covered likewise with gilded brass. The entire roof of the church is covered with sheets of brass.[6] The portico rests upon a platform of stone, which is raised five feet above the level of the street, and reached by steps all around the three sides. The front of the church is separated from the street by a narrow space, surrounded by an iron gate resting on a low stone wall and interrupted in five places by gates, two of which lead to a beautiful passage-way paved in brick, which runs all around the church and is destined for processions; the other three lead from the street to the church steps.

Inside the church is:

In the first place, the Sanctuary, four feet higher than the floor of the rest of the church. It is 40 feet long and 30 wide, and is separated by Corinthian balusters, which form the communion rail, reached by several steps running all the length of the sanctuary. The back of the sanctuary is decorated by four fluted columns, with their gilt capitals, an architrave, a frieze and a cornice, all of Corinthian style; in the pediment above is an oval window before which was placed a transparent picture representing under the form of a dove, emitting on all sides rays of light, some of which lose themselves in clouds in the midst of which may be seen many angels; on either side of the pediment is the gilded figure of an angel carrying the two tables of the Old and the New Law respectively. The organ loft is placed on one of the sides of the sanctuary; and on the opposite side is a gallery destined for the children of the orphanage. Underneath these two galleries are the doors giving access to the two side sacristies. The picture of the main altar represents our Lord crucified, with the Blessed Virgin, St. John and the holy women at the foot of the cross. This picture impresses greatly the Protestants who see it. The altar is of stone, and is covered with *antipendia*. A beautiful altar of marble, in

5. Removed about a century ago. They probably were packed with oily rags and ignited, partly for illumination, mostly for ornamentation.
6. The original roof finally was removed in 1876.

keeping with the church would be much to be desired; but the Bishop is unable to procure it, as he has still quite a few thousands of dollars to pay in order to extinguish the debt remaining on the edifice.[7] The walls of the sanctuary are marbled and ornamented with much taste by a young French painter, who is quite happy in the devising of these ornaments and very skillful in executing them.[8] He will paint the whole church.

The two side chapels with their altars next arrest our attention. These two chapels are on the same level as the sanctuary and the sacristies. They are decorated with two Ionic columns with gilded capitals, which support an architrave, frieze, cornice and pediment of the same style. The one is dedicated to St. Vincent de Paul, secondary Patron of the Diocese, and the other to St. Patrick, the Apostle of Ireland.

Underneath the sanctuary, the side chapels and the sacristies is a large underground chapel, measuring 84 feet in length and 30 feet in width.[9] It may be reached from the two side aisles of the church by two flights of stone steps; and likewise from the two sacristies and from the outside. This chapel is consecrated to the Blessed Sacrament; it is also destined for the administration of the Sacrament of the Penance, and for this purpose four handsome confessionals have been placed there. On solemn feasts when the Bishop officiates pontifically, Terce is chanted in this chapel and the celebrant puts on there his pontifical vestments. There also are the stations of the Way of the Cross. Hence it will be a place where the faithful shall be able to cultivate and exercise their devotion without distractions. Although this chapel is five feet under ground, yet it is well lighted by means of six windows.

To return to the church above, its main body is made up of three aisles divided by two rows of five columns; these are of brick covered with stucco and tinted so as to imitate marble; they measure 27 feet in height and 3½ feet in diameter; the capitals, which are of stone painted in brass finish, the architrave, the frieze and the large cornice running along both sides of the nave, are Doric. The vault of the nave soars forty feet above the floor; it is in the shape of a surbased arch, and divided in eighteen rectangular panels corresponding to the spaces between the columns, each decorated with cornice rose and other ornaments of stucco. The ceilings of the two side aisles are likewise stuccoed and painted so as to figure panels. The church is lighted by fourteen large windows sixteen by eight feet, semicircular in the upper part; there are also a number of other smaller windows, semicircular, oval or rectangular. All

7. The first of quite a number of hints to be found in this narrative.
8. Probably Leon Pomerede, who executed the sketch found elsewhere in this book. Church accounts cite a "Leon Commarecle," evidently the same person.
9. The installation of a massive marble altar in 1893 necessitated a brick foundation. The excavated dirt was left in the chapel. Only a crawl space exists today, but paintings on the plaster near the ceiling still are visible. The area is not open to the public.

will receive curtains fixed on hinges capable of moving at the least breath of the wind so that air circulation be not impeded; on these curtains will the principal scenes of the life of our Lord be depicted. This will supply the want of pictures, and at a glance the faithful will have brought to their minds what their Divine Redeemer deigned to suffer for men's salvation, and thus they will be excited to greater devotion. Alongside the wall in front are several spacious galleries for the use of the people; these galleries are so arranged that the men will be separated from the women, the boys from the girls. Attention was also given to the accommodation of the poor Negroes; for their special use are two beautiful galleries, where the persons of both sexes belonging to this class may assist separately at the divine offices. Finally, a handsome recess closed by an iron gate contains the Baptismal Font at a short distance from the church door. It must be confessed that this Baptismal Font is not altogether worthy of the new church; a marble Font would contribute not a little to the dignity of the administration of the Sacrament; but if Divine Providence does not furnish it, we will not have the means of getting it. There have been provided six holy water fonts, placed, according to custom, at the sides of the three doors. The sacristy is furnished with beautiful cases for the sacred vestments; unfortunately, the vestments which we possess are for the most part rather worn out and scarcely usable. The pulpit, located by one of the columns in the middle of the church, is of varnished wood, and of quite an elegant shape. Two hundred pews, disposed regularly in the body of the church, and a number of others in the various galleries, offer to the Catholics of the city, and to the Protestants who come with pleasure and in goodly numbers, the necessary accommodations to hear comfortably the word of God and the expounding of the dogmas of the Catholic religion. As winter here is quite rigorous, there were constructed in the basement two furnaces on the model of the heating apparatus invented recently and used successfully in various cities of this country; thus the furnaces are out of sight, and the hot air is let into the church by means of two circular openings, two feet in diameter, covered with a metal grate; the cost of heating is very little, owing to the abundance of coal in this country; and thus are removed the pretexts and excuses of those who invoked the severity of the weather to dispense themselves from coming to church.

The new Cathedral is alongside the residence of the Bishop, from which it is separated only by an alley eighteen feet wide.[10] The diocesan priests residing in St. Louis and exercising the parochial ministry with the Bishop, live with him a kind of community life, with its rules, its regular exercises of piety, spiritual conferences, reading of Holy Scripture at table, etc. Their life is one of retirement from all useless relations with seculars, from whom they never accept any invitations either to dinner or to supper

10. Replaced in 1852 by a rectory, which in turn was razed in 1961.

outside the house, so that they may always be ready for any calls. Their number is still inadequate to the needs, which in this city are harder to satisfy than elsewhere, because the population speaks three languages, French, English and German. A large number of German Catholics have come, and are continuing to come, to settle in the Diocese and the city of St. Louis. As a rule, they are very pious, industrious, and they do honor to the religion which they profess by word and deed. It is therefore necessary to preach in these three languages; yet all the clergy employed in the service of the parish at present consists only of the Bishop, two priests and a cleric. From time to time a Jesuit comes from the College to preach in English; and on solemn feast days, these Fathers come to help for pontifical functions.

On the west side of the Cathedral there is a beautiful piece of ground belonging to the church,[11] which might overwise have been turned into a source of revenue; however, in order to obviate the inconvenience resulting from having living houses so near the church, the Bishop has reserved this piece of property for the Orphan Asylum. The charity of the faithful is much interested in these children, of whom after the outbreak of the cholera twenty-five were gathered together and are raised in a small house; a fair held by the most respectable ladies of the city in view of the Orphanage has returned $1,000, besides $800 for the building of a new asylum. Providence will certainly do the rest. Building operations for this new Orphanage will commence next spring. Thus shall the infant Church of St. Louis follow at least from afar the examples given by the first Churches of the world from the earliest Christian centuries in the particular care they took of the poor, the orphans and the sick. These orphan boys housed near the Cathedral will be very useful as altar boys and will supply the wants of clerics.

The above is but a rough description of the new Cathedral. There is still a great deal to do, in order to finish the ornamentation, to acquire sacred vestments and other things necessary for the decency of the worship; and yet a great deal more in order to finish the payment of the cost and reimburse the loans made.

II. Solemn Dedication of the Church

The twenty-third Sunday after Pentecost, which in this year 1834 falls on the 26th of October, was the day chosen for the consecration of the new Cathedral. Of whatever might contribute to the magnificence of this august ceremony, nothing was omitted. The Bishop of St. Louis had invited the Right Rev. B. J. Flaget, Bishop of Bardstown, Ky., and the Right Rev. J. Purcell, Bishop of Cincinnati, Ohio, to grace the day by their presence. Then, learning that these two prelates were to celebrate about the same time at Bardstown another consecration not less solemn,

---

11. Long since deeded to the city for widening of Third street; still more for the expressway.

53

namely, that of the Right Rev. S. G. Bruté, Bishop elect of Vincennes, Ind., he requested them to have this ceremony coincide with that of the consecration of the Cathedral, and to come to St. Louis to anoint the new Bishop. The three prelates kindly condescended to this request, and at once set out on their journey, and in company with a priest crossed Indiana and Illinois and arrived in St. Louis on the 20th of October. All the missionaries of the Diocese who could do so came likewise from their various missions, to the Episcopal city for the appointed day, as also Rev. Fr. De Theux, Superior of the Jesuits, with his Novices, the Rector of the College and University of St. Louis with all the Fathers of the Company, and other ecclesiastics who teach there. There came besides the priests of the Congregation of the Mission who run the Seminary, College and University of St. Mary's of the Barrens, with other priests teaching there and a delegation of the students, as all, on account of the distance, were unable to reach here. Even from far away Kentucky had Father Petit, Jesuit, and the Rev. Abell, Pastor of Louisville, journeyed hither, who edified much of the people by their preaching, the one in French, and the other in English.

Meanwhile everything was in motion both in the city and in the neighborhood, without distinction of sex or religion, in view of contributing to the preparation for the feast or of being present thereat. The ladies and young ladies of the city vied with one another in bringing to the sacristies the objects they had wrought with their own hands for the ornamentation of the altars and the divine worship. Others exercised their voices which were to be heard in the new temple. Others again stripped their houses of carpets, candelabra and other rich pieces of furniture to decorate therewith the sanctuary for the solemnity of that memorable day.

There are in St. Louis three companies of militiamen, composed of the best manhood of the city. Each company is distinguished from the others by rich standards, and by special uniforms, all quite elegant. Of the individuals forming these companies some are Catholic and the other Protestant; for the present the three captains happen to be Protestants. At the mere mention made by a citizen of his own accord that the presence under arms of the three companies at the ceremony would contribute not a little to the solemnity of the day and to the maintenance of good order, the officers informed the Bishop that they were all willing to come, if he found it agreeable. The prelate did not fail to avail himself of these good dispositions. He sent them an invitation, which was most graciously acknowledged. Other men of the city wished to form for this occasion a corps of artillery; they had themselves drilled for a number of days by an army officer with very good results. Finally others requested and obtained the military band from the general commanding the U. S. troops at Jefferson Barracks, ten miles from St. Louis. A number of non-Catholic citizens declared in unmistakable terms that it was their set purpose that the feast should be celebrated with such pomp and solemnity that the memory of it should remain for many years to come.

Accordingly, on the Saturday eve of the celebation, despite a very heavy rain, the military band came from Jefferson Barracks; the artillery located itself in a place more convenient to announce in its own fashion the solemnity to the city and the neighboring country. Three bells, cast in Europe for the new church, one weighing 2,600 pounds, the second 1,900, and the third 1,300, were set in motion at 5 p.m., and their joyful pealings proclaimed the opening of the celebration. At once the artillery responded, and the military band joined its melodious notes to the majestic sound of the bells and the thunder of guns. At the sight of such a wonderful concourse in a city, a goodly proportion of whose inhabitants are not Catholic, and the joy which shone on every countenance, one would have sworn that in St. Louis there was only one worship, one religion, one faith, one flock and one Shepherd. At 6 p.m. the clergy, with the four prelates in their choir dress, went to the place where the sacred Relics were kept, and there recited Matins. The opening of the morrow's ceremony was announced for seven in the morning.

During the two or three days preceding that solemnity, the weather looked anything but favorable. A very heavy rain, accompanied by very strong wind, led to fear that the ceremony could not take place, or could take place only with great inconvenience. But about midnight the atmosphere unexpectedly cleared up, the clouds disappeared, and the skies could be beheld in their most gorgeous blue, studded with most brilliant stars. One could not wish for a more propitious day.

At the appointed hour (the) clergy assembled with the prelates in the Bishop's house, whence, accompanied by a guard of honor, they went in procession to the sanctuary of the old church, where the Relics of the Holy Martyrs, destined for the consecration of the altar, were inclosed in a nice gilded urn placed on a throne adorned with columns, above which was resting a sumptuous crown. The whole was decorated with draperies, festoons and garlands arranged most tastily and elegantly. Then the clergy, the prelates and the celebrant, preceded by the band and escorted by the guard of honor, walked to the main door of the new church, where a great assembly of people of the city and other places were already gathered to witness the grand ceremony. There also were arrayed in good order the men of the militia. It is useless to rehearse here all the rites prescribed by the Roman Pontifical; suffice it to note that everything was carried out to the letter. Meantime the crowd was constantly increasing; it was immense indeed. Religious silence reigned through it all, and every one seemed to await with awe the solemn moment when the doors of the temple would open at the voice of the consecrating Prelate. This moment arrived at length after the repeated prayers and rites which mark the blessing of the church on the outside. Three times had the whole clergy, following the Bishop, gone around it; three times had it stopped before the door, there redoubling prayers and sacred chants in order to obtain a happy entrance into the monument; three times also had the Pontiff struck the door with his crozier, pronouncing these grand words: *Attollite portas,* etc. At the third command at last the door was opened with stately solemnity before the Bishop and the Ministers, who alone are to witness the blessings of the edifice on the inside; and then it closed again.

The second part of the ceremony lasted about three hours, during which the crowd outside, instead of diminishing, continued to become larger. They were not left to languish during these long hours. Two Missionaries in succession from a raised platform gave, the one in French, and the other in English, a detailed explanation of the august ceremonies performed first in their presence, and then actually taking place inside behind closed doors, and also of those which the people were to witness when they would be permitted to enter into the church. These explanations were listened to with great attention, satisfaction and profit. At the completion of the sacred rites accomplished inside the church, the consecrating prelate, the other Bishops and all the clergy, preceded by the militia and followed by the guard of honor, went in procession, accompanied by the strains of the band, to the old church, to bring the Relics. After the chanting of the Responses and the other ceremonies prescribed by the Pontifical, the procession retraced its steps towards the new church in the following order: First, part of the militiamen; then, marching by two, twenty altar boys in red cassocks and immaculately white surplices, followed by twenty clerics of the Seminary, the College, or the Jesuit novitiate, behind whom were thirty priests. (A remarkable illustration of the catholicity of the Church could be drawn from the fact that these priests were of seven different nationalities.) Finally came the sacred Relics, carried on their little throne by four priests; and behind the three Prelates with their attendants and the consecrating Bishop with his own ministers. The militia closed the triumphal cortege, which progressed with becoming majesty through the immense crowd of people. More beautiful and impressive spectacle had never been beheld in these parts; nothing more capable of inspiring a holy and religious awe and respect towards the Supreme Ruler of the universe, for whose worship and in whose honor this pageant was enacted, than the serious and solemn chanting of the liturgical hymns, the harmonies of the military band, accompanied by the majestic peal of the bells and the loud thundering of the cannon, which together fell upon the ears of the spectators. Arriving at the Cathedral, the procession marched around it with the sacred Relics. It stopped at the main door, whilst the Bishop was tracing upon the latter which Holy Chrism the sign of our redemption. Finally the Consecrator, the other Prelates, the clergy and the people entered with the sacred Relics of the Holy Martyrs into the new temple. In such circumstances the eagerness born of curiosity is wont to cause disorder and disturbance in the crowd. But thanks to the wise arrangement of the militia, to their attention and to their activity, the church was filled without trouble and confusion; and in a few minutes everybody was at his place, and all could with religious attention witness the ceremony of the consecration of the altar. The two sections of the band, placed before the side altars, now played alternately, and now blended their melodious chords in triumphal hymns which resounded under the arches of the temple. From time to time they gave place to the organ which, from one of the galleries of the sanctuary, accompanied the voices of the sacred ministers and of the people uniting to sing the praises of the Lord. The august spectacle of this sacred ceremony, this almost heavenly harmony, left no time for piety to flag, or for the attention to weary. All the senses were at the same time engaged in holy occupations. Which goes to prove that our senses were given us by the Creator to raise our souls to Him by means of the exterior objects which strike them; and that the Catholic religion finds in the majesty of its ceremonial, according to the intention of its Divine Founder, and turns wisely to advantage one of the most active and powerful instruments furnished by nature to express in a sensible manner to her children invisible and supernatural realities, which otherwise they would not be able to discover and to understand.

The consecration being now finished and the ornaments of the altar blessed, the ministers adorned the altar with candlesticks and reliquaries containing the precious Relics of the Holy Apostles. In the meantime the officiating Bishop, the Prelates and all the clergy went down to the lower chapel to put on the sacred vestments for the celebration of the Holy Mass; and coming back in orderly procession went through the nave and reached the sanctuary. The priests had donned chasubles, the celebrant's ministers cope and dalmatics, the Bishops likewise cope and mitre, and the celebrant the customary pontifical vestments. The Pontifical Mass was celebrated by the Bishop of St. Louis with all the ceremonies prescribed in the Ceremonial of the Bishops. The music, written by an Italian composer living in St. Louis and executed by volunteer singers who form the regular choir of the Cathedral, proved worthy of the solemnity of that memorable day. The militia under arms with their flags unfurled assisted at the celebration of the holy sacrifice. Several guardsmen, placed at the foot of the altar and at the entrance of the sanctuary, rendered the honors to the sovereign Ruler of the universe and to the Lord God of Hosts. When came the moment when, at the tremendous words of the consecration pronounced by the celebrant, the Word made man came down for the first time in his new temple as the unbloody victim offered in behalf of men, all the bells tolled solemnly, the cannon roared and the band instruments modulated their sweetest melodies; and at once the militiamen bent their knees to the floor, the military flags in humble homage were lowered to the ground, and the whole people, Catholics and Protestants alike, yielding to the irresistible impulse of sacred awe, prostrated themselves before the majesty of the Hidden God, the Victim of propitiation offered up for their sins. Who would not wish to be a Catholic at such a moment?

After the Gospel, Bishop Purcell, of Cincinnati, ascended the pulpit, and first announced in English and French that every morning of the octave solemn mass would be sung, at which a French sermon would be preached, and every evening about nightfall Solemn Vespers were to be chanted and followed by an English sermon. He then began a most eloquent discourse in English on this text: *God alone is great.* He developed admirably this thought, applying it to the ceremony of the day, so well calculated to bring home this greatness of God, which transpires through all the works of the Creator; and then he turned most happily to this other idea: *And man too, is great,* delineating in most vivid colors the characters of true greatness, which religion alone is capable of communicating to man by uniting him with God by means of the worship which He demands of His rational creatures.

The Pontifical Mass finished at 3 p.m. and the crowd went home, their hearts filled with the most pure joy, and incapable of speaking of anything during the rest of the day except what they had seen, heard and felt in the holy place. This still continues to be the general and frequent topic of conversations both in public and in private. May God make use of it to bring to effect His merciful designs on many who had the opportunity of becoming acquainted with the Catholic Church, listening to the explanation of her true dogmas; and may He lead some to come to the knowledge of the truth! Already some among them have had their eyes opened to the light of truth which illumined them, and are preparing to return to the bosom of the Church. It was a source of no mean satisfaction to the Bishop of St. Louis, who, a few days later was traveling in a steamboat with two priests, and was not recognized, when he heard with his own ears a man of good judgement, who had declared he was not a Catholic, defending against some others who were attacking the Church, her dogmas, her practices and her people in a manner which would have done credit to the most learned priest.

Pontifical Vespers were celebrated at 6 p.m. by Bishop Flaget, Senior Bishop of the United States, assisted by other Prelates and all the clergy, and were followed by an English sermon preached by Fr. Abell. The preacher, still under the vivid impression which he had experienced in the morning on seeing the American militia, who had spontaneously offered their services and so nobly comported themselves, began by declaring he could find no words to express adequately the sentiments which overflowed from his heart; then he exclaimed: "Today I have beheld for the first time the militia of my country assembled in a body to render solemn homage to the old religion of our fathers; today I have beheld for the first time the brave defenders of our liberties presenting their swords and bending down their heads before the altar of Christ; today I have beheld for the first time the noble flag of my country inclining respectfully and saluting the tabernacles of the living God. Ah! May such a solemn homage, the sincerity of which cannot be suspected, since it was all spontaneous, become for us a salutary and comforting earnest of the union of all American minds and of all American hearts in the same faith and the same worship, just as all are animated by the same love and the same zeal for the same country and the same laws." He then thanked the companies of the militia in the name of the Bishop and of all the clergy. On the next day the three captains, all the officers and a number of men of the militia came together to the Bishop's residence to thank him for the favor he had bestowed upon them by accepting the concourse of their services for this august and solemn ceremony. Such was the conclusion of that truly religious feast, the precious remembrance of which will long remain engraved in the memory, and still more in the hearts of the people of St. Louis.

On the day following the consecration, and on the other days of the octave, Mass and Vespers were solemnly sung, with a sermon in French and English morning and evening respectively, as had been announced; they were attended by the four Bishops and the clergy who still remain in St. Louis. Both the Bishop of Bardstown and the Bishop of Vincennes preached several times in French; and their sermons full of unction edified very much the people. Every evening at six o'clock the Church was grandly illuminated, and was filled with Catholics and Protestants, who were coming to attend Vespers and the sermons on various controversial subjects touching the notes and the qualities of the Church of Jesus Christ. These instructions, given in a spirit of charity and with eloquence and clearness were received with pleasure and great profit.

On the 28th, feast of the glorious Apostles Simon and Jude, took place the solemn consecration of the Right Rev. Simon Bruté, Bishop of Vincennes. Bishop Flaget was the consecrating prelate, having for his assistants the Bishops of St. Louis and of Cincinnati. At this occasion the Bishop of Cincinnati preached a most eloquent sermon. He proved with most cogent arguments, and clearly demonstrated the divine institution of the Episcopate; he enumerated the advantages accruing from it, showed the wonderful fecundity with which it was endowed by its divine founder, the number of the institutions which originate from it. All this was explained by the orator in a manner well calculated to strike his listeners and to make, as it were, more palpable to them the truth of his assertions. He depicted for them in vivid colors as in a bird's eye view the history of what has been accomplished most wonderfully in the course of the few years elapsed since the erection of the first Episcopal See in the United States, and particularly since the division of these immense regions into various Dioceses, since the time still recent when Bardstown, Cincinnati and St. Louis welcomed their first Bishops; he rapidly as by so many masterly strokes of the brush presented before their eyes the ecclesiastical and religious foundations, the communities of priests and of sacred Virgins, the schools, the universities, the colleges, the seminaries, the orphanages, hospitals, convents, churches and cathedrals. None of those were in existence before the Episcopate came to fertilize these regions still but recently desert and barren, and to plant and propagate and extend by their daily exertions the true religion of Jesus Christ.

One the first of November, Feast of All Saints, Bishop Purcell officiated pontifically. The round of solemnities was concluded the following Sunday by solemn Mass and Vespers chanted by Bishop Bruté. In the evening the concourse of people was extraordinary. There was exposition of the Blessed Sacrament, during which *Te Deum* was sung to thank God for the great benefits bestowed upon the city of St. Louis. After the Benediction, the Blessed Sacrament was carried in procession to the lower chapel and placed in the tabernacle of the altar destined for the dwelling-place of the Hidden God, and consecrated to his special worship. We fondly hope that, thanks to the peace and tranquility which in His goodness and mercy He will deign to accord to this Church as yet in its infancy, He will be pleased to reside there for centuries to come, and to receive the homages of the faithful souls that, despite the perversity of this age, in which faith is weakening and charity grows cold, He never fails to raise to Himself, as in all times and in all places He finds delight among them, *Deliciae mea esse cum filiis hominum.*

✝   ✝   ✝

On midnight of April 6, 1835, fire broke out in a livery stable, spread to the old church, and burned it out. Flames from the stable licked at the upper windows along the north wall of the new Cathedral, but it was saved by the sheet brass roof and a timely change in the wind.

On September 22 that same year, Rosati made a fateful entry in his diary: "I invited to dinner the workmen and others who had cooperated in the building of the church."

A man as decisive as Rosati could scarcely be expected to be without enemies; who they were isn't known, but they lost little time in capitalizing on the dinner Rosati held for the laborers.

After more than a year had elapsed since receipt of the once-regular contributions from the Society for the Propagation of the Faith, Rosati concluded that word of his "extravagant banquet" and other like "reckless expenditures of money" had been reported to Europe. In 1836, he wrote: "I never suffered so much in my life ... for the last two years I have received nothing from Austria; and yet never at any time have my needs been more pressing than this year ... I am at a loss as to the means of having my letters reach the Leopoldine Institutions ... It was reported at Lyons that I need no help, live in a house whose appointments are shockingly luxurious, and keep for myself all the money sent ... With the sole exception of a dinner which I gave to the workmen who built the Cathedral,

60

and cost me $20, the only persons who have ever sat at my board are the priests who happen to be in St. Louis."

The appeal evidently was effective, for shortly thereafter the contributions from abroad were resumed.

✝   ✝   ✝

Rosati, during one of his infrequent trips abroad, gained an audience with Gregory XVI, his classmate, and asked for the Cathedral the indulgences[12] attached to the seven Basilicas of Rome. The Pontiff objected, stating that these indulgences were reserved only for persons visiting the Seven Basilicas in the Eternal City. That Rosati eventually was successful in his plea is evidenced by the Pontifical decree of April 3, 1841:

Holy Father:

Joseph Rosati, Bishop of St. Louis, humbly prostrate at the feet of your Holiness, asks that your Holiness deign to grant in perpetuity, the usual conditions being observed:

1. A Plenary Indulgence daily to the faithful visiting the Cathedral Church of St. Louis.

2. The Indulgences of the Seven Churches of Rome to those visiting the four (now attached to the three) altars of the said Cathedral Church.

3. The Indulgences of the Stations of Rome to those visiting the said Cathedral Church on the days of such stations.

4. A Plenary Indulgence on the anniversary of the dedication of same church and during the octave of said dedication and on the octave day.

5. A Plenary Indulgence on the Feast of St. Louis, the Patron of the Cathedral Church, and throughout the octave.

6. A Plenary Indulgence on the Feast of St. Vincent de Paul, and also on the festivals of his death and the translation of his relics and during the octaves.

7. A Plenary Indulgence on the Feast of St. Patrick and throughout the octave.

8. A Plenary Indulgence to all youths of both sexes of all the parishes in the diocese of St. Louis on the day of

---

12. For our readers who are not Catholic, an Indulgence is the remission of the whole or part of the temporal punishment due to sin.

their first communion; also to those of their parents who shall receive Holy Communion on that occasion.

9. A Plenary Indulgence to all the faithful of the diocese on the day on which they receive the Sacrament of Confirmation, having first received Holy Communion.

10. A Plenary Indulgence on the Festival and throughout the octave of the dedication of every church of the Diocese of St. Louis, either already consecrated or hereafter to be built and consecrated.

11. A Plenary Indulgence on the festival and throughout the octave of the patron saint of each church of the diocese, already erected or to be erected.

12. That priests who are in parishes or missions of the diocese may gain the said and any other indulgences although because of the want of a confessor they do not approach the Sacred Tribunal of Penance.

The reply to the petition reads as follows:

In an audience with His Holiness, held on the third of April, 1841, our Most Holy Lord, Gregory XVI, by Divine Providence Pope, on the statement of the undersigned Secretary of the Sacred Congregation of the Propagation of the Faith, having considered the matter of the petition, graciously grants in perpetuity all the indulgences asked for in the petitioning brief. All things to the contrary notwithstanding.

Given at Rome from the offices of the said congregation, on the day and year as above, entirely free from any remuneration under any head.

J. Archs. Edessen.

Chapter VII

ST. LOUIS MISSIONS IN THE WEST

It is altogether fitting that The Old Cathedral should be integrated, physically if not legally, into the Jefferson National Expansion Memorial. From a period of 1826 until 1843 the territory administered by the St. Louis diocese exceeded by far that of the Louisiana Purchase. The western and southern boundaries were contiguous with the western border of Idaho, bisecting vertically the state of Nevada, continuing eastward along the northern borders of Arizona, New Mexico, Texas and Louisiana. The eastern border was the Mississippi up to its juncture with the Ohio, then northward through the center of the states of Illinois and Wisconsin. The north border was the Canadian line.

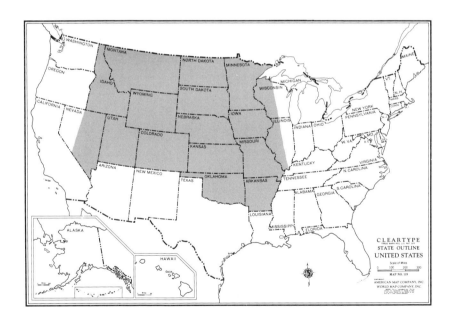

TERRITORY ADMINISTERED FROM THE OLD CATHEDRAL AT ONE TIME
ENCOMPASSED NEARLY HALF OF AMERICA.

Into these vast regions, the poor diocese of St. Louis managed to send priests, not only among the Indian nations displaced by treaty to reservations, but to the savages in the Trans-Rockies. Some of these expeditions were fabulously successful. Some were heart-breaking failures. The Jesuits found that in addition to fighting ignorance, they had to combat the white man's firewater; and in some cases it was too much.

In 1820, Du Bourg was visited by a company headed by Sans-Nerf, a chief of the Osage, seeking a "Black Robe" to instruct them in the Catholic faith. The savages were described as follows: "Their copper-colored bodies were coated with grease, their faces and arms were striped in different colors, white lead, vermilion, verdigris, and other colors formed a great variety of furrows, all starting at the nose."

In 1821, Charles de La Croix journeyed by horse 12 days west of Florissant to meet the chief, who escorted him on a 10-day tour of the neighboring villages. La Croix found polygamy rampant; when a young brave married he automatically married all the bride's sisters. The lands of the Osage, long since inundated by the Lake of the Ozarks, were not particularly suitable to cultivation. But the nomadic Osage were too lazy to farm it anyhow. La Croix saw his prime obstacles to a successful mission the polygamous tendencies of the tribe, the whiskey being traded for peltry by the white man, and the "itinerant minister."

Du Bourg, however, realized that there was much to be done with the Indians, and was well aware of his inability to provide the missionaries with which to do it. He petitioned for a group of Jesuits in 1821, offering a tract of land at Florissant.

The Jesuit contingent—two priests, seven novices, and six slaves—arrived in the Spring of 1823, immediately set about building St. Stanislaus. A school for Indian boys opened in May of 1824, and at about the same time Mother Duchesne opened her Sacred Heart school for Indian girls.

The Master of the Novices was Charles Felix Van Quickenborne, a Belgian. Among his novices was young Peter De Smet, who was to go down in history as "the greatest Indian missionary of our age."

Van Quickenborne visited the itinerant Osage tribe on three occasions between 1827 and 1830, as they migrated in southeast Kansas, near Fort Leavenworth and Fort Scott.

It was in May, 1827, that a delegation of the heathen Kansas Indians—the descendants of the same tribe visited by Coronado—visited Governor William Clark to obtain missionary help. Du Bourg sent Joseph Anthony Lutz, then 26, to their villages near the mouth of the Kansas river, the site of Kansas City. The energetic Lutz made a number of trips to the Kansas villages, and during the course of the next four years he also established temporary missions at Sangamon City (Springfield) and Galena, Illinois. He was in Prairie du Chien —where Marquette and Joliet first floated out onto the Mississippi— in 1831, when a band of marauding Fox Indians ambushed his Memonies, killing 30. Lutz fled, eventually returning to St. Louis to become assistant pastor to Saulnier; finally pastor of the St. Louis Cathedral from 1831 to 1844.

The Jesuits continued their activity in their vast dominions between the Missouri and Mississippi. They were in Jefferson City in 1828, in northwestern Missouri, Council Bluffs (across the Missouri from Omaha), Sugar Creek and St. Mary's in Kansas. Felix Verreydt went to Louisiana, Missouri, in the Salt River country. Van Quickenborne in 1832 penetrated central and northern Illinois, then back to Florissant through the Salt River settlements. In one year alone, this devoted missionary traveled 4,373 miles, most of it alone.

In 1829, President Andrew Jackson won legislation to relocate Indian tribes of the East, which were on the verge of extinction by the encroaching whites, in lands not yet committed to statehood. The Ottoes, Omahas and the Prairie (Iowa) Potawatomies were located near Council Bluffs, and a tribe known as the Kickapoos were relocated in Eastern Kansas, a few miles above Fort Leavenworth. On June 1, 1836, Van Quickenborne started a mission school of logs for the Kickapoo boys. The little log building measured 16 feet by 15 feet, had one window, one door, and 20 children. An old log cabin became a chapel. A house was built for the missionary priests, two stories, 18 feet by 49 feet.

In 1835, Van Quickenborne paid a visit to a mixed band of Indians—the Peorias, Weas, Piankeshaws, and the Kaskaskias. These were the same Kaskaskias who, led by Gabriel Marest, left their ancient village for River des Peres, then on downstream to the village of Kaskaskia.

"An old woman, whose gray hair and bent-up form showed that she had belonged to by-gone times, crawled up to the missionary, grasped his hand with a strong expression of exultation and pronounced him to be a true black-gown, sent to instruct her hapless and neglected nation. She had lived at least a score of winters longer than any other of her tribe, but yet she distinctly remembered to have been prepared for her first communion by one of the Jesuits who attended the flourishing mission of Kaskaskia. She gave a description of the old church, recited her prayers and sang a Canticle in the

65

language of the tribe.

Another mission was established to the north—among the Pota-watomies along the Missouri, near Council Bluffs. Verreydt and De Smet received from Col. Kearny a blockhouse to use as their church. The Indians contributed four cabins for use as schoolrooms and dwellings.

PETER DE SMET

The young missionaries could more than hold their own against the devil, but demon rum proved to be quite another adversary. Quoting De Smet's celebrated diary:

"They give horses, blankets, all, in a word, to have a little of this brutal-izing liquid. Their drunkenness only ceases when they have nothing more to drink . . . In all directions, men, women and children are seen tottering and fall-ing; the war-whoop, the merry Indian's song, cries, savage roarings, formed a chorus. Quarrel succeeded quarrel. Blows follow blows. The club, the tomahawk, spears, butcher knives, brandished together in the air."

"June 3rd. (1838) A woman with child, mother of four young children, was murdered this morning near the issue-house. Her body presented the most horrible spectacle of savage cruelty; she was literally cut up.

"June 4th. Burial of the unhappy woman. Among the provisions placed in her grave, were several bottles of whiskey. A good idea, if all had been buried with her.

"June 6th . . . I know from good authority that upwards of eighty barrels of whiskey are on the line ready to be brought in at the payment."

The mission was abandoned in 1841.

Late in 1831, a group of four Indians arrived in St. Louis—Man of the Morning and Black Eagle, chiefs; and two young braves named No Horns on His Head and Rabbit-Skin Leggings. They had ob-viously come from afar, and it was several days before a person could be produced capable of translating their strange tongue. These were braves of the Nez Perce nation, known as "Flatheads." They were in search of a "Black Gown" for their village, near the Pacific Ocean. The hot summer climate wreaked havoc with their health. The two chiefs died in St. Louis, shortly after they were baptized. After it was explained that at the time there simply were no missionaries to give them, the remaining pair left for their home. Both died before reaching their village.

A second delegation of Flatheads—a man and his two sons—returned in 1835 to repeat the request. They were advised that as soon as a missionary was available he would be sent to them. On their return, the old man was ambushed by a Sioux band and killed.

A third expedition came shortly thereafter, and was overjoyed to hear that their new missionary was Peter De Smet. De Smet and one of the young braves left Westport (Kansas City) in 1840, to cross the American desert and the Rocky Mountains. De Smet left livid accounts of the passage—the fastness of the Wind River region, the majestic mountain peaks, the lush valleys, or parks. They met the welcoming party somewhere near the Continental Divide. On July 10, they reached the headwaters of the Columbia, and shortly thereafter were in the camp of the Flatheads—1,600 souls.

On New Year's Eve he arrived back in St. Louis, but the following Spring kept his word and returned with five other missionaries to build his mission on the banks of the Bitter Root river.

De Smet in his lifetime traveled more than 180,000 miles in the American West, and crossed the Atlantic 16 times (usually in search of support for the missionary activities.) Few, if any, of the legendary mountain men knew more about their country than did this courageous Black Robe, nicknamed "Samson" by his classmates in his seminary days.

He was well known and trusted by the Indian—he is credited with the success of the council at Fort Laramie in 1851, with the settlement of the Mormon War and Yakima War of 1858-59. His most daring exploit occurred in 1868. Sitting Bull had sworn to kill all white men on sight, a pledge regarded by the stocky cleric as downright uncharitable. De Smet rode directly into his camp in the valley of the Big Horn and persuaded the feared chieftain to smoke the calumet.

Chapter VIII

ST. LOUIS UNIVERSITY

Although Du Bourg had a "college" of his own, his main educational interest was theological, not secular. Thus, when the need became apparent for an institution of higher learning in the St. Louis area, he asked that the Jesuits do something about it, with his cooperation. Thus was the beginning of St. Louis University.

Van Quickenborne was apprehensive about Du Bourg's suggestion, and asked that he relay it to the Maryland Superior. Du Bourg had, meantime, found an angel—the generous Irishman Jeremiah Connor, who had laid out Washington avenue through his land.

He offered two lots, but died before the commitment could be set to paper. Jesse Lindell bought them for $210 under the sheriff's hammer, but Van Quickenborne stepped in and offered to trade another lot for the 270-foot piece on Washington, between Ninth and Tenth streets. The offer was accepted.

The school was opened on November 2, 1829, with an enrollment of 10 boarders and 30 day students, which quickly swelled to 150 students. On December 28, 1832, the school was raised to "St. Louis University" by act of the State Legislature.

The University today is one of the most distinguished in the nation, with its present enrollment of 10,000 expected to hit 15,000 in a few years. It has expanded to fill much of the mid-town area around Grand and Lindell boulevards with several new buildings, and many more on the way.

Chapter IX

KENRICK—YEARS OF TRIUMPH AND TRAGEDY

Almost a quarter-century had elapsed since young Rosati left Rome for the New World—all of them years of hard work and most of them years of triumph. He began, therefore, to look forward to a rest, and a visit to Rome and his native Sora. After devoting a year to the visitation of practically all the churches in his sprawling diocese, Rosati left for Europe. In May, 1840, he arrived at the residence of the Bishop of Philadelphia, Francis Patrick Kenrick. There he met the Bishop's younger brother and Vicar-General, Peter Richard Kenrick. "Admiring more and more his piety, knowledge and modesty and his other virtues, I was inspired with the desire to obtain him from the Holy Father as my Coadjutor."

In Rome, where young Kenrick had already made an impression, Rosati gained an affirmative answer, and Kenrick was installed on November 30, 1841. He arrived in St. Louis a month later.

The appointment of Kenrick as his coadjutor was made to free Rosati to attend a matter of the Vatican—that of restoring the Catholic Church on the island of Haiti. After devoting a year to that purpose, he sailed again for Rome, on February 22, 1843, to make his report to the Pope. He was in Paris, ready to return to St. Louis, when a recurring pulmonary disturbance prompted him to return for the air of his native land. There he died, on September 25, 1843.

It was through the efforts of Archbishop Joseph Elmer Ritter of St. Louis that his body was returned from the Vincentian cemetery in Rome. His remains were interred in the New Cathedral in 1956, in the same crypt as Glennon's.

✝   ✝   ✝

Rosati probably didn't suspect it, but his request for Kenrick as his coadjutor was to result in a fiscal solidity that endures to this day in the Archdiocese.

PETER RICHARD KENRICK

And had Kenrick known of the sorry condition of the exchequer at the time of his appointment he no doubt would have refused the honor. Rosati had left an indebtedness of $58,000.

The congregation of the church was something less than apathetic. A meeting of the city's prominent Catholics, during which those in attendance were asked to sign pledges, produced a total of $25, from one person only. The Bishop adjourned the meeting politely, declaring, "Gentlemen, I will dispense with your services for the future. I will adopt some other means of paying the debt."

Rosati had leased the northern half of the church block and now Kenrick decided to develop most of the remaining ground not actually in use for church purposes.

On the tract facing Second street he erected a group of commercial buildings for $36,231. He sold these in 1853 for $182,602. When the old orphanage was removed from Third and Walnut streets in 1851 he erected there a group of combination business-residential properties for $19,086. It was sold for $75,250.

Then he started a bank, capitalized by the savings of the prudent Catholic workmen of the area. Wise investments returned additional thousands. The new rectory was built and paid for. A brick addition to the north end of the church served as a sacristy and a three-floor parochial school. The chapel beneath the Sanctuary was closed and the floor lowered to its present position.

✝   ✝   ✝

When Kenrick came to St. Louis in 1841, the city had a population of 30,000 people, more than half of whom were Catholic. The population was doubling each decade; more than 500 immigrants were added to the Church rolls annually. Had all the Catholics attended Mass the church would have had to hold 15 services every Sunday.

On Easter Sunday, 1843, the Church of St. Francis Xavier was opened near the Washington avenue campus of St. Louis University. September 15, 1844 saw the opening of Our Lady of Victories on Third and Gratiot street in south St. Louis. St. Patrick, on Sixth and Biddle, still stands. It was opened May 4, 1845. St. Vincent's was opened in November, 1845.

There now are nearly 250 churches within the boundaries of the St. Louis Archdiocese, plus a number of mission churches in St. Louis and St. Louis County.

Just as the Old Cathedral parish became smaller so that the Diocese could better serve St. Louis Catholics; so it was that the Diocese had to become smaller to accommodate the Catholics of the West.

In 1837, Rosati petitioned the Vatican to establish a diocese which would become known as Dubuque, across the Mississippi and downstream from the mouth of the Wisconsin.

Milwaukee, Little Rock, and Chicago were given diocesan status in 1843. In 1850 St. Paul became a diocese and Kansas City, Kansas, became a vicarate-apostolic. Omaha became a vicarate-apostolic in 1857, and Denver, with the missions of the Trans-Rockies, followed suit in 1868. That same year, St. Joseph became a diocese. All the above except Little Rock and St. Joseph have since been awarded archdiocesan status.

71

Subsequent dismemberment of the old St. Louis diocese: Kansas City, Missouri, 1880; Oklahoma City-Tulsa, 1905; Jefferson City, 1956; and Springfield-Cape Girardeau, 1956.

The current boundaries of the archdiocese run from Elsberry, on the river 50 miles north of St. Louis, to the mouth of Apple Creek, where Du Bourg first said Mass in his diocese, about 85 miles downstream. It forms an irregular semi-circle to the west, out as far as Hermann, 65 miles west. Besides the City of St. Louis, it embraces the counties of Perry, St. Francois, Ste. Genevieve, Washington, Jefferson, Franklin, St. Charles, St. Louis, Warren and Lincoln—all of which have a Catholic population of about 500,000.

In 1833, a French lawyer named Antoine Frederic Ozanam and seven companions founded the St. Vincent de Paul Society, dedicated to service to the poor. The Old Cathedral is the home of the society in America.

TABLET COMMEMORATING SOCIETY OF ST. VINCENT DE PAUL, MOUNTED ON SOUTH WALL OF THE OLD CATHEDRAL.

Bryan Mullanphy had become familiar with the Society while studying in France. In 1845 he assembled a group of prominent Catholic laymen in the old college building and established the first council of the St. Vincent de Paul Society in America.

The organization still fulfills its original function—in St. Louis, America and the world.

St. Louis had her good years and she had her bad ones too. The worst year on record—perhaps for any city—was 1849, when mother nature dealt the sprawling rivertown a two-part calamity.

St. Louis was asking for cholera. De Smet described the conditions of 1849: "Imagine a city, of 70,000 inhabitants, crowded and packed together in new brick houses, in the dampest and worst drained prairie in existence, undulating, imperfectly drained and interspersed with sink-holes and stagnant waters. The city has hardly

72

a sewer, and in the new streets, mostly unpaved, all the offal of the horses runs out or is thrown out in the omnipresent mud. Add to this that outside the center of the corporate limits is a dirty pond (Chouteau's Pond, on the site of the present Union Station), a mile or more in circumference. Around this natural 'slop bowl,' at short intervals, you find breweries, distilleries, oil and white lead factories, flour mills and many private residences of Irish and Germans, into this pond goes everything foul—this settles the opinion as to the real cause of all the dreadful mortality here."

It all started just before Christmas, 1848, when a steamer pulled into the bustling riverfront from New Orleans. Between her passengers and crew there were 30 cases of cholera. Ravaged with nausea and diarrhea, they mingled freely in the riverfront saloons, hotels and restaurants.

There were "one or two" fatalities reported in a January 9 edition of a daily newspaper; a total of 36 deaths were reported in that month. The number for February declined to 21, climbed to 78 in March. After 128 deaths were reported for April, the citizenry began to be alarmed.

A Committee on Public Safety was formed to try various remedies, including the burning of oily rags, feeling that the fumes would destroy the poisoning in the air. They set aside June 2 as a day of fasting and prayer.

The members of the growing Society of St. Vincent De Paul left their comfortable homes to administer what help they could to the wretched victims.

The seven priests of the city worked day and night. Despite their state of continual exhaustion, not one was claimed by the disease. The good sisters of St. Louis Hospital would not be so fortunate. The seven sisters worked day and night to save the lives of 820 of the 1,330 cholera patients who had come to them. Two of them gave their own lives to the cause. Other religious orders, too, gave what they could to comfort the sick and dying. The plague claimed two Sisters of St. Joseph, one of the Visitation order, and six from Sacred Heart.

The downturn started in late July, and only a few fatalities were reported in mid-August. By the time the epidemic had run its course, it had taken 4,317 of the citizens to their graves. For a two-month period alone, Catholic burials were averaging 20 a day.

Strangely enough, there wasn't a single case reported among the faculty or student body of St. Louis University, probably due to the fact that their wells remained uncontaminated.

✝   ✝   ✝

The epidemic was beyond question the worst, but not the only, tragedy in the city's bicentenary history—the loss of seven per cent of the population, gouged indiscriminately out of the social structure, was a deep and damaging blow. But at the height of that plague the city was to sustain yet another calamity, fatal to only three, but carrying away $10,000,000 worth of income-producing property.

At about 9 p.m. on the night of May 17, fire was reported aboard the steamer *White Cloud,* tied up at the foot of Cherry street, on the northern fringe of the downtown riverfront. The hope of saving her was quickly abandoned, and her moorings were cut to allow the current to take her to midstream where she would burn out. But a spanking northeast wind kept her from moving to the east, and the current drove the floating holocaust against the other boats along the levee. Bumping one, then another, she destroyed 33 boats in all. The blaze jumped the levee at Locust street, moving due south. Then it moved up a block to First street, and as it crossed Market, it was up to Second, the church block.

Since the entire riverfront was an inferno, the volunteer fire brigades had no place to turn for water. Thomas B. Targee, choirmaster of Christ Church (Episcopalian) and captain of the Missouri Valley Fire Brigade, elected to blow up a number of buildings in order to form a fire break. He dispatched wagons out to the St. Louis Arsenal to bring in several kegs of gunpowder.

Protecting the kegs from sparks with damp tarpaulins, he blew up first one, two, and three buildings, all around the windward side of the Old Cathedral. He entered a music store on Market street, two doors down from the church block, the last building that could transmit the fire to the west. The keg blew up in his hands. It is the Protestant Targee that St. Louis Catholics must thank for the existence of their old church on the riverfront.

✝   ✝   ✝

THE OLD CATHEDRAL WAS ONE OF VERY FEW RIVERFRONT BUILDINGS TO
SURVIVE GREAT FIRE OF 1849.

For several years before and after the twin calamities, St. Louis was in the grip of an emotional tragedy, the advent of nativism, or the "Know-Nothings."

During the 1840's, this movement was concentrated largely against the new immigrants, particularly the Irish, who seemed to have a penchant for political power. In St. Louis, that meant that the Catholic church had to bear some of the brunt of the attack, for the new Irish were almost 100 per cent Catholic. At one time the nativists advocated a 25-year residence as a requirement for citizenship and holding public office.

The movement manifested itself largely in election day riots, although scattered incidents were reported throughout a decade. During one such riot, in 1854, an inflamed band of Know-Nothings set out for Third and Walnut streets, determined to sack and burn the Old Cathedral. But a grizzled old Irishman, a veteran artilleryman from Waterloo, had moved a large brass cannon just outside the front door. At the sight of it, the band lost much of its determination and, turning on its heels, lofted a few rifle balls through the gilded cross high above Walnut. The wave of bigotry was ended.

✝   ✝   ✝

THE OLD CATHEDRAL IN
1840s – DAGUERREOTYPE
TAKEN FROM THIRD STREET
LOOKING TOWARD RIVER.

The Old Cathedral, hemmed in on all sides by commercial buildings, was well into her period of decline as a parish by 1860. The city was moving north, south and west—only the commercial enterprises remained along the river. In November of 1860, Kenrick adopted the new Church of St. John the Apostle as his Pro-Cathedral.

While the old parish itself was entering into a period of decline, the opposite was true with the diocese. It became the first archdiocese west of the Mississippi river on July 20, 1847. Peter Richard Kenrick, who had overcome the spectre of bankruptcy, proved a wise and capable leader of his flock. Throughout the tide of nativism and open bigotry, he urged calm on the troubled city. During the bloody rioting over the slavery-secession issues in 1861, he issued this injunction:

"In no case is a Christian justified in forgetting the precept of universal charity . . . Listen not to the suggestions of anger, but banish from your thoughts as well as from your hearts every feeling incompatible with the duty of subjecting it to the dictates of reason and religion. Remember that any aggression by individuals or bodies not recognized by the laws from which the loss of life may follow is an act of murder of which everyone engaged in such aggression is guilty, no matter how great the provocation may have been. 'Dearly beloved, let us love one another.'"

Kenrick died on March 4, 1896, at the age of 89. This once-brilliant archbishop was so broken of mind by 1893 that his successor, John Joseph Kain, had to be appointed in that year.

Chapter X

KAIN, GLENNON, AND A NEW CATHEDRAL

JOHN JOSEPH KAIN.

It was Kain who laid the groundwork, in 1896, for the structure that would replace The Old Cathedral as the cathedral of the St. Louis Archdiocese. On October 28 he issued a pastoral letter announcing the selection of the block bound by Newstead, Taylor, Maryland and Lindell boulevard, for this purpose. Thus was begun a building process which was to extend almost a full 60 years. He died after a lingering illness on October 13, 1903. Subtracting the years of his own illness, and that of Kenrick, he was able to devote only five years to his Archdiocese. But things were in good order for the arrival of John Joseph Glennon.

☩   ☩   ☩

JOHN CARDINAL GLENNON.

John Cardinal Glennon became the first Archbishop of St. Louis to become a prince of the church. But a St. Louis bursting with pride was never to see its new Cardinal. Breaking his return journey from Rome with a visit to his native Ireland, he died in the home of the President, in Dublin, March 9, 1946 at the age of 83. His body lies in All Souls crypt in his cathedral.

Glennon was appointed coadjutor to Kain on April 27, 1903. He was only 41 when he became archbishop of St. Louis. His sparkling wit soon made him St. Louis' most popular Irishman.

77

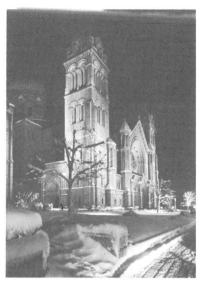

THE NEW CATHEDRAL, NEWSTEAD
AND LINDELL. BEGUN 1908,
COMPLETED 1966.

Anxious to begin work on his great Byzantine cathedral, he awaited the close of the World's Fair to start the solicitation of the necessary funds. The cornerstone was laid October 18, 1908, and the building was opened for worship exactly six years later. It was dedicated June 29, 1926.

During Glennon's administration a total of 85 churches were built in the city and St. Louis County. He built almost as many schools, and his new Kenrick Seminary opened in 1915.

By the time of his death, the St. Louis Archdiocese had grown to become one of the most impressive in the United States.

THE OLD CATHEDRAL IS HEMMED IN ON ALL SIDES IN THIS 1927 PHOTO.

78

Chapter XI

CARDINAL RITTER—THE ERA OF RENEWAL

Kenrick in 1870 attended the Vatican Council in Rome, the first ecumenical meeting since the famous Council of Trent, 300 years before. There he was a highly respected member of a minority which questioned the timeliness of the promulgation of the dogma of Papal infallibility as being both unnecessary and inexpedient. Kenrick's position was defeated, but his views were so crisply defined that he was urged by some to pursue the matter. While his disappointment was acute, he refused to take any further action.

JOSEPH CARDINAL RITTER
Courtesy St. Louis Review

There are some parallels to be drawn between Kenrick's courageously liberal stand and other events which occurred nearly a century later, at the Second Vatican Council. *The New Yorker Magazine* described "Joseph Cardinal Ritter, of St. Louis, the smiling, cheerful archbishop who, for all the simplicity of his approach, turned out to be the outstanding American prelate at the Council." The magazine referred to the St. Louis Archbishop's studied eloquence during the 1962 session.

The Cardinal is one of the influential members of the Council. He was a member of the 110-man Central Preparatory Commission for the Council; was elected to the Conciliar Commission for the Discipline of the Clergy and Laity; and was appointed by Pope Paul VI a member of the Post-Conciliar Consilium for the implementation of the Constitution on the Liturgy. He is one of two American Bishops appointed to this last body which is charged with the revision of the Mass and Sacraments of the Catholic Church.

Active in all sessions of the council, he took a leading role during the 1964 session in such issues as religious liberty, the role of the laity, Christian education, a review of Church laws on mixed marriage, and a statement on the relationship of Christianity to non-Christian religions and especially to the Jews.

As there are parallels, there also are contrasts. St. Louis owes its early diocesan beginnings to Du Bourg's fear of entering what was to have been his see city of New Orleans, due to the crafty Sedella.

Archbishop Ritter was in his see city only one year when his own mettle was tested. The ramshackle old St. Joseph's High School for Negroes was about to collapse. Instead of building a new structure, he elected to integrate the pupils in the archdiocesan high schools, and at the same time desegregate all other Catholic schools. The Archbishop sent a letter to all pastors informing them of this move.

The tempest quickly outgrew the teapot. A group of 700 white parishioners from 23 north side parishes raised a fund of $400 to retain legal counsel and, if necessary, file an injunction to prevent integration of their schools.

One of their officers was applauded when he said, "If His Excellency the Archbishop wants schools for Negro children, we will build them. But we do not want colored and white children together in the schools and we will not have it."

The Archbishop was to mince no words in dealing with the recalcitrants:

"After mature deliberation, and fully confident of the loyalty of the faithful, we now deem it opportune to caution them publicly. By the general law of the church, there is the serious penalty of excommunication, which can be removed only by the Holy See. This penalty is incurred automatically should an individual or group of individuals, without permission, in violation of Canon 2341, presume (that is, with full knowledge) to interfere in the administrative office of their bishop by having recourse to any authority outside the Church."

The leader of the dissidents capitulated. "I personally will not take any action that will jeopardize my religion or that of anyone else."

The revolt was over. There were to be no others.

The Archbishop was soon to be heard from again, in other areas of brotherhood. A wealthy west St. Louis suburb had been selected by Rabbi Ferdinand Isserman's Temple Israel congregation as the site of its new temple. Zoning restrictions were hastily enacted to prevent such a move. Both Archbishop Ritter and the Metropolitan Church Federation (of Protestant churches) backed the Jewish cause.

It was this same Metropolitan Church Federation which, late in

1964, elected to cite the Cardinal as their "Ecumenical Man of the Year." He declined the honor because "it is associated with the performance of what I consider my simple duty." The MCF then stated that they would not give the citation to any other person. "In our hearts we shall have honored you in lieu of an outward symbol."

Eden Seminary, the graduate school of theology of the United Church of Christ, conferred on Cardinal Ritter its honorary doctor of divinity degree, on June 4, 1965.

"As far as we know, this is the first time that a cardinal of the Roman Catholic Church will have addressed the graduating class of a Protestant seminary," stated Dr. Robert T. Fauth, president of the seminary.

The doctorate was awarded "in recognition of Cardinal Ritter's active participation in the promotion of understanding and good will among people of all faiths."

Archbishop Ritter was proclaimed a Cardinal by Pope John XXIII at the Consistory of January 16, 1961.

The son of a baker, he was born July 20, 1892 in New Albany, Indiana, and spent the first 52 years of his life in that state. He became the first archbishop of Indianapolis in December 1944. He was appointed archbishop of St. Louis July 20, 1946.

Chapter XII

RENAISSANCE

Luther Ely Smith, a St. Louisan, was a member of the commission to develop a memorial to George Rogers Clark at Vincennes. While serving in this capacity, he had one of the truly great ideas of our time. "If that can be done in Vincennes," he reasoned, "why can't something much bigger be done in St. Louis?"

He spelled out his plan to Mayor Bernard F. Dickmann (who was married in The Old Cathedral). Dickmann stated he would back the plan provided it received the endorsement and support of the civic leaders. On December 15, 1933, Dickmann called a meeting in the Jefferson hotel. The business leaders were reminded that some 40 blocks of the downtown riverfront had fallen into abject decay, because the city had turned its back to the river that gave it birth. Smith encouraged the men to promote the 82-acre tract between Poplar street and Eads bridge, west to Third street, as a national monument.

The Jefferson National Expansion Memorial would commemorate Thomas Jefferson, under whose presidency Louisiana was purchased, and the pioneers who broke open the American West and gave America claim to her natural boundaries.

President Franklin D. Roosevelt authorized the Department of the Interior to acquire the ground, in cooperation with the citizens of St. Louis. The only exception—and the only building to be saved—was The Old Cathedral, gradually achieving historical importance. (The Old Courthouse, officially part of the Jefferson National Expansion Memorial, stands two blocks west of the main tract.)

After delays caused by innumerable controversies and two wars, ground was broken on June 23, 1959. Work on the 630-foot stainless steel arch began in April, 1962, and was completed early in 1966. The legs, located above Grande Rue, or First street, are 630 feet apart. The south leg is just 150 yards northeast of the Old Cathedral.

The national Park Service, the supervising agency for the memorial, estimates that the Gateway Arch, and the vast Museum of Westward Expansion buried beneath and between the legs, will attract upwards of 3,000,000 visitors a year to St. Louis.

✝   ✝   ✝

At the time of the inception of the plan, The Old Cathedral was

CENTURY-OLD RECTORY (ABOVE LEFT) AND THREE-STORY ADDITION TO CHURCH ITSELF AS THEY APPEARED SHORTLY BEFORE DEMOLITION IN 1959. NOTE HEAVY TREATMENT OF CHURCH WINDOWS. VIEW FROM SAME DIRECTION NOW REVEALS DISCIPLINES OF GOOD ARCHITECTURAL DESIGN, AT WORK TO EMPHASIZE BEAUTY OF ORIGINAL BUILDING.

surrounded by decay. Blocks of old buildings surrounded the church —most of them in ruination. But as demolition proceeded, the citizens of St. Louis became aware once again of the sturdy old structure which, with the tottering old rectory, stood alone on the historic site.

While the building itself was sound, it had fallen victim to well-meaning remodelers of 1876. The delicate windows had been ravaged by thick iron mullions, totally out of character with the architecture of the church. The massive marble altar for which Rosati longed, erected finally in 1893, overpowered the entire nave. The oval window had been plastered over with the addition of the school to the north wall, and the broken pediment converted to a full pediment, adding to the towering awkwardness of the sanctuary. The nave was dark and musty-looking. The only sparkling thing about the interior was an electric sign on the pediment. The Old Cathedral, in sum, hardly reflected the grace with which the Catholic Church had prospered in the century since the church was built.

MASSIVE 1893 ALTAR BLOCKS OVAL WINDOW. LEGEND WAS OUTLINED WITH SMALL ELECTRIC BULBS.

On St. Patrick's Day, 1959, four years after his appointment as pastor of the Old Cathedral, Msgr. James E. Hoflich was given the task of supervising a complete rehabilitation of the church.

✟   ✟   ✟

It is under the pastorate of Msgr. Hoflich that the old church is seeing her greatest glories, eclipsing those of Rosati's time both spiritually and secularly. During that time it became a Basilica by pontifical decree. It has fulfilled the spiritual needs of hundreds of thousands of people. And it has achieved a temporal beauty far superior to that of the original.

Fr. Hoflich, born in Kentucky in 1906, spent his youth near the present approach to MacArthur bridge. He was serving as administrator of St. Raymonds Church of the Maronite rite when he was appointed pastor of the Old Cathedral in 1955. A year later he was named a domestic prelate with the title of Right Reverend Monsignor, and shortly after was appointed to the additional post of Secretary for Education for the St. Louis Archdiocese.

The first job of the rehabilitation program was to commission in 1959 the noted firm of Murphy and Mackey as architects. Then began an exhaustive program of research to isolate the design and construction details of the church as it was built originally.

It was the conclusion of all persons concerned that an absolutely faithful restoration would be neither practical nor in the best interests of those St. Louisans who had attended services there for decades. For instance, replacement of the stone candelabra above the parapet would detract from the distinguished but simple architecture of the original structure. There obviously would have to be some minor interior adjustments to accommodate the air conditioning. The cost of duplicating the original box pews would be prohibitive and would cut the seating capacity somewhat. There was no reason to restore the below-ground chapels, so they have been left as they were.

The replacement of the aged brick rectory appears from the river to be a plain garden wall, bending around the rear of the building where it encloses the new sacristy. Thus, for the first time in a century, virtually all of the four walls of The Old Cathedral are exposed for public admiration.

It is interesting to note that, as the old school addition was demolished and the oval window once again exposed to daylight, the workmen found the sill in near-perfect condition. On it was a pencil sketch of a girl's head, with the inscription, "Mat Hastings put 4 lights in window, Nov. 18, 1851." (Hastings later became a noted painter of the American West.)

The research indicated that there were very few statues in the original church. All agreed that far too much statuary—most with little relation to the church itself—had been accumulated over the past 125 years. Much of it was removed, to keep the building more in harmony with the evident intent of Rosati.

The heavy old altar and reredos were removed, and replacements in keeping with the scale of the building—believed to be a duplicate of the original—were installed. The four original columns were re-mounted in the original position, and now a broken pediment handsomely frames the oval window.

85

ARCHITECT JOSEPH D. MURPHY (TOP) AND CONTRACTOR DON C. MUSICK EXAMINE
ANCIENT WALNUT BEAMS IN ROOF STRUCTURE. ALL WERE FOUND TO BE SOUND.

Because of the scale of the interior, the architects elected to
utilize pewter and silver leaf extensively. Combined with French
blue, white and magenta carpet, the church now imparts a light and
delicate appearance.

A careful examination of the intricate empire-styled mouldings
and ceiling ornaments indicates they almost certainly were imported
from France. They were treated with silver leaf. The windows have
been returned to the original Georgian design. The floor and joists
were perfect, needing only stripping and finishing. The throne has
been rescaled and reupholstered, in line with the Cardinalature
rank of the Archbishop.

The stone on the sides of the building, probably quarried a few
yards away on the riverfront, was found to be in perfect condition,
and did not even require tuckpointing.

✝   ✝   ✝

Rosati, in his description of the painting above the main altar,
said it "represents our Lord crucified, with the Blessed Virgin, St.
John and the holy women at the foot of the cross. This picture
impresses greatly the Protestants who see it."

THIS 108-YEAR-OLD INSCRIPTION WAS FOUND ON SILL OF OVAL WINDOW WHEN IT WAS "RE-DISCOVERED" IN 1959 —"MAT HASTINGS PUT 4 LIGHTS IN (THIS) WINDOW NOV. 18, 1951." BENEATH DATE IS SKETCH OF GIRL'S HEAD.

The plaster beyond the central panel of the altar revealed traces of such a painting, evidently rendered in distemper. This is a temporary substance made by mixing pigments with glue size.

The architects determined that the rehabilitation program should include a painting in the same position—only one of more artistic consequence than that depicted in the lithograph prepared by the original decorator of the church, Leon Pomarede.

Working with Charles F. Quest, an art Professor at Washington University, they assembled prints of a dozen great crucifixion paintings by such masters as Velazquez, El Greco, Titian and Rubens.

Cardinal Ritter himself selected "The Crucifixion" by Diego Velazquez, as the one to be duplicated for The Old Cathedral.

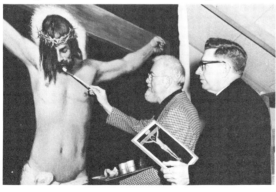

MSGR. JAMES E. HOFLICH, PASTOR OF THE OLD CATHEDRAL, COMPARES PRINT OF VELAZQUEZ' "THE CRUCIFIXION" WITH OUTSIZE COPY BEING COMPLETED BY CHARLES F. QUEST.

The original painting was executed between 1628 and 1639, after a commission by Philip IV of Spain, and given by him to a convent of Benedictine nuns to which the church of San Placido belonged. It hung in the sacristy there, then passed into private hands, and finally was purchased by King Fernando VII, in whose reign what is now the Prado Museum was built.

"The painting has been much debated by art authorities," according to George McCue, art editor of the *St. Louis Post-Dispatch*. "It is argued that the detailed realism of the matted hair partly covering the face and the blood streaming from the wounds is inconsistent with the relaxed and almost comfortable appearance of the body. It is in the manner of presenting the image, glowing and almost seeming to float in its dark space, that the painter achieved mastery of his theme."

Quest said that the painting fit The Old Cathedral better than any of the other great works which were under consideration. "The painting has a very spiritual and devotional approach. It is not as gory as some of the others, and it depicts the figure of Christ by Himself."

Quest made a small copy of the painting, plus two other Velazquez works, to help develop the master's technique. The artist flew to the Prado in Madrid for detailed oil sketches of the original, in order to capture its "subtle qualities."

The Quest work, measuring eight feet by fourteen feet, is about 30 inches wider and 50 inches higher than the original.

✝ ✝ ✝

In 1961, Pope John XXIII, through the Sacred Congregation of Rites, decreed basilican status upon the church previously known as the Church of St. Louis IX, King of France. The official name of The Old Cathedral now is the Basilica of St. Louis, the King.

The following is an edited summary of the official decree:

JOHN XXIII

AS A PERMANENT RECORD OF THE FACT

In St. Louis, an industrial city in the State of Missouri, is the illustrious Church of St. Louis, the King, formerly its Cathedral, built by contributions of its congregation and their neighbors during the Pontificate of our Predecessor, Pope Gregory XVI * * * This venerable temple of God * * * is recognized as an important center of Religion from which, as from a headquarters, the Catholic Faith was carried to the surrounding regions. * * * This Church, since it is situated in a business section of the city, has become a sort of Shrine where the downtown St. Louis community comes for services and private prayer. The staff of Clergy assigned to the Church is, as it should be, sufficient in number for carrying

out solemn Religious functions with proper decorum. With all these facts in mind, our beloved son, Joseph Elmer Ritter, Cardinal-Priest of the Holy Roman Church, Archbishop of St. Louis, asked us to endow this Church of such outstanding importance with the name and title of Minor Basilica. Being favorably disposed to this petition, after consultation with the Sacred Congregation of Rites, We, with full knowledge and mature deliberation by the plenitude of our Apostolic Power by virtue of these letters, do raise for all time to the dignity of a Minor Basilica that Church in the City and Archdiocese of St. Louis consecrated to God in honor of St. Louis, the King, with all honors and privileges which pertain by law to Churches honored with this same title, conflicting claims of whatever kind having no validity. We publish and establish these things decreeing that the present letters shall stand firm, valid and effective continually for all time * * *

Given at St. Peter's, Rome, under the Ring of the Fisher-

PAPAL DECREE DESIGNATES THE OLD CATHEDRAL AS BASILICA. SMALL CIRCULAR AREA AT BOTTOM IS IMPRINT OF "FISHERMAN'S RING" OF POPE JOHN XXIII.

man, the 27th day of the month of January, the year 1961, the third year of our reign.

BASILICAN CONOPOEUM—12 FEET HIGH—OF THE OLD CATHEDRAL . . . COAT OF ARMS OF POPE JOHN XXIII IS AT LEFT, THAT OF JOSEPH CARDINAL RITTER IN FOREGROUND.

/s/ D. Card. Tardini
Office of Public Affairs

There are only a few churches in the world with higher honors. The major basilicas of Rome are St. John Lateran, St. Peter's, St. Pauls outside the Walls, and St. Mary Major.

In canon law, the term "basilica" denotes a distinguished church upon which either ancient custom or papal decree has bestowed the name as a title of extreme honor.

A basilica is granted certain ornamental privileges over its sister churches. The two invariably communicated are the right to display a basilican conopoeum (translated as either "pavilion" or "umbrella"), and a tintinnabulum—a small bell mounted

BASILICAN TINTINNABULUM, "LITTLE BELL," IS CARRIED IN PROCESSIONS.

upon an elaborate frame.

The conopoeum is a large symbolic umbrella, never more than half-open, therefore conical in shape. Its red and yellow silk stripes are encrested with the coats of arms of John XXIII, Cardinal Ritter, Rosati (as builder of the church), and the official basilican seal of The Old Cathedral. The stem of the conopoeum is actually a carrying pole, topped with an orb and a cross. It is 12 feet tall.

93

The tintinnabulum is six feet in height, carved of wood in an elaborate baroque style and ornamented with gold leaf. The bell itself is relatively small—six inches at the mouth—and is rung only when it is carried in processions. The frame is crowned with a carved papal tiara and keys.

Both the conopoeum and tintinnabulum are constantly on display in the nave of The Old Cathedral.

The significance of the high honor of basilican status may escape visitors who are not Catholic, but it is the only reward which would be fitting to a wilderness church which at one time nursed half a continent to spiritual maturity.

Only 16 other American churches presently hold Basilican status. The seal was prepared in Rome, and described as follows:

It should be said in advance that inasmuch as we have to do with a Coat of Arms not for a single person or a family but for a legal entity, such as a Church, we should speak of a "seal" which follows the rules proper to sphragistics which are different from those of heraldry.

These are:

1. Among the many heraldic symbols decorating the present Coat of Arms, preference was given to those which had some connection with the life and the times of the titular Saint of the Basilica.

2. Now St. Louis, King of France, as a member of the ancient house of Valois used a flag of blue "sown" with golden lilies (the reduction to only three lilies to one is much later). Also, Prince Charles, brother of the King and Count of Anjou, gave to his realm a Coat of Arms "sown" with lilies of gold (Fleurs de lis) of France. Also many ancient cities and guilds of French artists and artisans had at their head the same heraldic device.

3. The form of the Lily of France preferred in the present case is the most ancient one used by Charles and consequently contemporary with St. Louis.

4. The blue field was selected for the following historical reasons: the red top (sown with golden lilies) as a matter of fact, was restricted to the pennant or "great shield" placed above the royal pavilion.

5. It was not believed either opportune or necessary to divide the shield into two parts or fields of which one on the side of honor (to the left of the person looking at the shield)

assigned to the Coat of Arms of the Archdiocese of St. Louis as is customary with Archbishops. The Basilica of St. Louis of France is now no longer the Cathedral. Consequently, it would not be correct from a juridical point of view to incorporate in the Coat of Arms the Coat of Arms of the Archdiocese.

6. The two red conch shells placed at the top of the shield are intended to indicate the two Crusades in which St. Louis participated (he died in the second). The conch shells, whether they be the Spanish shell of St. James or the French shell of St. Michael, are a symbol of the Crusades.

7. The shield is oval as is proper for an ecclesiastical entity.

8. The shield bears as a crest the Basilical "Ombrellone" tied with red and gold ropes from which hangs the "Tintinnabulum" proper to Basilicas.

BLAZON: A blue field sown with golden lilies of France. At the head, a field of silver bearing two convex conch shells of red.

✝ ✝ ✝

The period of reconstruction was long and arduous. At times it was difficult for the devout to see the celebrants because of the maze of scaffolding and building materials. Yet, attendance grew steadily. Noon Mass on holidays often finds every seat taken, with the faithful jammed into the aisles. As the tide of visitors to the memorial increases, the attendance at the old church grows steadily. Five masses are said every Sunday.

Thus, The Old Cathedral has survived the transition from a parish-cathedral church in a small frontier community, to cathedral of a massive local diocese, to ex-cathedral status, to parish-without-parishioners, and finally has emerged as one of the focal points of a great national monument.

As the Jefferson National Expansion Memorial commemorates the great men who welded a wild continent into the United States, so this humble old church now is being revered by men of all faiths, from all over the world, as the fountainhead of spiritual fortitude of an earlier day.

JOSEPH CARDINAL RITTER
Archbishop of St. Louis
and the seal of his
Cardinalature.

ST. LOUIS, THE KING. LOUIS IX OF FRANCE, ONE OF A NUMBER OF PAINTINGS
PRESENTED TO DU BOURG BY LOUIS XVIII.

BISHOPS WHO HAVE PRESIDED OVER THE
OLD CATHEDRAL AND PREDECESSOR CHURCHES

Bishop Joseph Rosati   Archbishop John J. Kain
Archbishop Peter R. Kenrick   Archbishop John Cardinal Glennon
        Archbishop Joseph Cardinal Ritter

PRIESTS WHO HAVE SERVED AT THE OLD CATHEDRAL
AND PREDECESSOR CHURCHES

PASTORS

P. F. Bernard de Limpach	1776-1789	Francis Kielty	1863-1865
Jean Antoine Le Dru	1789-1793	Louis Dold, C. Ss. R.	1866-1868
Dom Pierre Jos. Didier	1794-1799	Myles Tobyn	1868-1886
Pierre Janin	1800-1804	Eugene Coyle	1886-1915
Thomas Flynn	1806-1808	John J. Tannrath	1915-1922
Felix De Andreis	1818-1819	Paul C. Schulte	1922-1937
Francis Niel	1819-1825	Mark K. Carroll	1937-1942
Edmund Saulnier	1825-1831	John W. Marren	1942-1945
Joseph A. Lutz	1831-1844	Walter J. Tucker	1945-1948
Simon Paris	1844-1857	Lloyd A. Sullivan	1948-1955
Patrick J. Ryan	1857-1860	James E. Hoflich	1955
Ralph Capezutto	1860-1863		

ASSISTANT PRIESTS

Leo De Neckere	1819-1829	John St. Cyr	1849
Fr. Dahmen	1819-1820	Stanislaus Bernier	1848-1850
B. Martial	1819	Michael Prendergast	1853
Leo Deys	1820-1823	William Wheeler	1853-1857
A. B. Anduze	1820	Patrick J. Ryan	1853-1857
Edmund Saulnier	1821-1825	James Duggan	1850-1854
Eugene Michoud	1823	Philip Kendricks	1858
Joseph Lutz	1825-1831	Myles Tobyn	1858
Francis Loisel	1828-1834	Michael McFaul	1859
A. Dussanssay	1828	John Hennessy	1859-1860
Angelo Mascaroni	1830-1831	J. S. Latour	1861-1862
Fr. Lefevere	1832-1835	Edward J. Fitzpatrick	1861-1862
Peter Doutreluigne, C. M.	1834-1836	David Phelan	1863
Philip Borgna	1834-1835	Patrick O'Neil	1863
James Fontbonne	1836-1844	Patrick J. Gleeson	1864
Francis B. Jamison	1836-1839	Michael Welby	1864-1865
J. Pierre Fischer	1836-1844	Francis Gallagher	1864-1865
Joseph Renaud	1836-1853	Egidius Smulders, C. Ss. R.	1866-1868
George Hamilton	1843-1844	Ferroel Girardy, C. Ss. R.	1866-1868
Benedict Roux	1842-1846	William H. Brantner	1868-1869
Ambrose Heim	1845-1854	Edward Fenlon	1869
John Higginbotham	1845-1846	Edward Shea	1869-1870
Edmund Saulnier	1847-1862	Martin S. Brennan	1870-1871

Edward Smith	1871-1872	Paul C. Schulte	1915-1922
Patrick McEvoy	1872-1875	George J. Donnelly	1922-1925
George Watson	1872-1874	Jacob A. DeMoor	1925-1939
David Doherty	1876-1877	Ambrose C. Winkelman	1939
Edward J. Dempsey	1877-1878	Vincent J. Mogelnicki	1939-1940
James Bourke	1878-1882	Justin J. Brauner	1940-1943
Edmund A. Casey	1882	Peter J. Rahill	1943-1945
James McMahon	1883-1884	John T. Ronquest	1945-1946
John White	1884-1885	James P. Mulderig	1945-1947
John Hughes	1885	Elmer H. Behrmann	1947-1949
Michael McFaul	1887	Louis F. Meyer	1949-1955
Arthur F. O'Reilly	1889-1890	John Daniel Moore	1953-1957
Peter J. O'Rourke	1890-1893	Lambert Hrdlicka	1955-1956
Richard Brady	1893-1894	Kenneth Jaas	1956-1958
John Tracy	1894-1895	Jerome F. Wilkerson	1957-1961
Joseph R. Watson	1895-1899	Richard J. Gallagher	1958-1959
Michael F. Taylor	1899-1904	Anthony G. Siebert	1960-1962
Joseph Casey	1904-1905	Bernard H. Geisman	1961
Denis P. Mulcahy	1905-1909	Robert G. Ditch	1962
Francis Schiller	1909-1915		

ALL PHOTOGRAPHY BY ARTEAGA ST. LOUIS, MO.

Lithographed by the James Mulligan Printing Co., St. Louis, Mo.

INDEX

101

INDEX—(Continued)

105

INDEX–(Continued)